# DIGITAL DESIGN THEORY

## READINGS FROM THE FIELD

Edited by
Helen Armstrong

PRINCETON ARCHITECTURAL PRESS
NEW YORK

Published by
Princeton Architectural Press
A McEvoy Group company
37 East Seventh Street
New York, New York 10003

Visit our website at www.papress.com

Printed and bound in China by 1010 Printing International
19 18 17 16  4 3 2 1 First edition

Design Briefs Series Editor: Ellen Lupton
Editor: Nicola Brower

Special thanks to: Janet Behning, Erin Cain, Tom Cho, Barbara Darko,
Benjamin English, Jenny Florence, Jan Cigliano Hartman, Lia Hunt,
Mia Johnson, Valerie Kamen, Simone Kaplan-Senchak, Stephanie Leke,
Diane Levinson, Jennifer Lippert, Sara McKay, Jaime Nelson Noven,
Rob Shaeffer, Sara Stemen, Paul Wagner, Joseph Weston, and Janet Wong
of Princeton Architectural Press  –Kevin C. Lippert, publisher

Library of Congress Cataloging-in-Publication Data
Digital design theory: essential texts for the graphic designer/
Helen Armstrong.–First edition.
        pages     cm
Includes bibliographical references and index.
ISBN 978-1-61689-308-8 (alk. paper)
1. Graphic arts–Data processing. 2. Commercial art–Data processing.
I. Armstrong, Helen, 1971- editor.
NC1000.5.D54 2016
41.60285–dc23
                                                2015027140

READY OR NOT, COMPUTERS ARE COMING TO THE PEOPLE.
THAT'S GOOD NEWS, MAYBE THE BEST SINCE PSYCHEDELICS.

STEWART BRAND
"Spacewar–Fanatic Life
and Symbolic Death Among
the Computer Bums"
1972

# CONTENTS

## SECTION ONE: STRUCTURING THE DIGITAL

## SECTION TWO: RESISTING CENTRAL PROCESSING

**90 THEORY AT WORK: 1980-2000**

## SECTION THREE: ENCODING THE FUTURE

**138 THEORY AT WORK: 2000-PRESENT**

BUILDING TOWARDS

A POINT OF ALWAYS BUILDING

## ACKNOWLEDGMENTS

Essential to this project, of course, are the many eminent designers who graciously contributed their work. Special recognition goes to Lenka Kodýtková, Radoslav L. Sutnar, Alberto Munari, Wim Crouwel, Jakob Bill, Laura Hunt, and Nicholas Negroponte for their help negotiating the maze of copyright permissions inherent to a project such as this. I would also like to express deep gratitude to Dr. Glenn Platt and Dr. Bo Brinkman for their continuing insights and to Peg Faimon, a wonderful designer, friend, and mentor. Without Peg's support, this book would not have been possible.

A special thanks to my students—Ali Place, Danny Capaccio, Ringo Jones, Kansu Özden, and Paulina Zeng—who provided a strong sounding board for this collection in the classroom, never failing to inspire through their own energy and creativity. At Princeton Architectural Press, my gratitude goes to my editor, Nicola Brower, for her thoughtful comments. Finally, thanks go to my husband, Sean Krause, for his patience, love, and editing skills, and to my daughters, Vivian and Tess, who remind me each day what this crazy life is really about.

# INTRODUCTION
## GIVING FORM TO THE FUTURE

Designers work at the crux of accelerating technological change. We spend so much time straining to keep up that we rarely have a moment to reflect upon how we got to where we are. How did we get here? How has computation brought us to this point? This collection attempts to answer these questions. Our story begins in the late mid-twentieth century: the 1960s.

In 1963 computer scientist Ivan Sutherland wrote a computer program called Sketchpad (also known as Robot Draftsman), through which he introduced both the graphical user interface (GUI) and object-oriented programming, proving that not only scientists but also engineers and artists could communicate with a computer and use it as a platform for thinking and making.[1] In the same year computer scientist J. C. R. Licklider, director of Behavioral Sciences Command and Control Research at the Defense Department's Advanced Research Projects Agency (ARPA), began discussing the "intergalactic computer network," an idea that fueled ARPA research and developed into the ARPANET, an early version of the Internet. Soon thereafter, in 1964, IBM released a new mainframe computer family, called System/360, a family of computers capable of meeting both commercial and scientific needs. It was the first general-use computer system. Four years later engineer and inventor Douglas Engelbart, assisted by Stewart Brand, conducted the so-called "Mother of All Demos," in which he presented the oN-Line System, a computer hardware and software system that included early versions of such fundamental computing elements as windows, hypertext, the computer mouse, word processing, video conferencing, and a collaborative real-time editor. Although mainframe computers were still inaccessible to most artists and designers in the 1960s and '70s, the idea of computation began to inspire visual experiments. The zeitgeist of the computer was in the air.

Two key inventions for designers—and indeed for everyone—happened in the incredibly fertile period that followed: the development of the Macintosh in 1984, the first personal computer sold with a GUI; and the creation of the Internet, used by academia in the 1980s and adopted for widespread use in the '90s. As we entered a new millennium, these two inventions became the defining tools of designers' practice, not just practically but also ideologically. The personal computer brought computation to the masses while the Internet networked both mind and information on a large scale. Since

1 Ivan E. Sutherland, "The Ultimate Display," *Proceedings of the IFIP Conference* (1965), 506–8.

the 1960s these tools have spawned technology-oriented approaches that continue to shift the foundations of our practice to focus on parameters rather than solutions, an aesthetics of complexity, and a culture of hacking, sharing, and improving the status quo. Now we move toward a fresh visual language, one driven not by gears and assembly lines but by connective tissues that bind the organic and the digital together.

## STRUCTURING THE DIGITAL (1960-80)

During the 1960s, programmers of mainframe computers had to clearly articulate and translate a series of logical steps into the unequivocal language of the computer. They fed these steps, the "program," into the machine using a punch card or punched tape. Artists and designers of the same period began to experiment with this idea by breaking down the creative process into set parameters and then structuring those parameters into a series of steps to be followed by either a human being or—theoretically at the time—a computer.

Manipulating a limited number of aesthetic parameters to enact a design project was not a new idea. Earlier in the twentieth century, avant-garde artists at the Bauhaus—and advocates of the New Typography movement that followed—developed the modular grid. Widespread codification and commercial application of this concept took off after World War II as designers including Josef Müller-Brockmann, Emil Ruder, Max Bill, and later Ladislav Sutnar and Karl Gerstner began to grapple with the onslaught of information thrust at them by mid-twentieth-century society. These Swiss style designers organized information into graphic icons, diagrams, tabbed systems, and grids that could be quickly comprehended by a busy twentieth-century citizen. The post–World War II industrial boom demanded that they develop such efficient systems for organizing and communicating information.

Grids, in particular, supported efficiency. Along with corresponding style guides, they allowed the designer to create new layouts by selecting from a limited number of choices rather than starting from scratch each time. This constraint sped up the process, encouraging designers to translate intuitive decisions into specific parameters such as size, weight, proximity, and tension. The result was a series of visually unified designs that could accommodate a wide variety of data.

2  Karl Gerstner, *Designing Programmes* (New York: Hastings House, 1964), 21-23.

In his 1964 book Designing Programmes Gerstner translated the resulting design parameters into a logical language that, he believed, a computer could understand and then combine and recombine to create design solutions.[2] The same year Italian designer Bruno Munari organized an exhibition titled Art Programmata for the Italian information technology company Olivetti. In the exhibition catalog Munari explained that programmed art "has as its ultimate aim the production not of a single definitive and subjective image, but of a multitude of images in continual variation." The desired end of a project was no longer a single solution but rather a series of "mutations."[3]

3  Bruno Munari, *Arte programmata. Arte cinetica. Opera moltiplicate. Opera aperta.* (Milan: Olivetti Company, 1964).

Many artistic movements delved into processes of input, variation, and randomization during the 1960s and '70s: concrete art, serial art, op art, the New Tendencies movement, conceptual art. Sol LeWitt's Wall Drawing series is one of the most familiar examples. For each drawing, LeWitt devised a set of instructions to be followed by another human. "All of the planning and decisions are made beforehand," he explained, "and the execution is a perfunctory affair. The idea becomes a machine that makes the art."[4] In this way, the instructions are the core of the project: the algorithm. An assistant, full of his or her own subjective intuition, completes the project by following the instructions. LeWitt builds unique iterations into his system through the subjectivity of each human participant. This focus on crafting parameters and randomizing input to produce a variety of solutions—rather than just one perfect form—privileges behaviors over static relationships of form and meaning. Such behavior-oriented systems were precursors to interactive design approaches in the 1980s, the '90s, and beyond.

4  Sol LeWitt, "Paragraphs on Conceptual Art," *Artforum* 5, no. 10 (1967): 79-83.

Alongside these process-oriented artistic movements, the counterculture exploded in the United States during the 1960s and '70s, questioning traditional modes of authority over such sweeping political issues as civil rights, the Vietnam War, feminism, and the environment. Proponents began to envision what society could become through social engineering. Stewart Brand's Whole Earth Catalog, part magazine, part product catalog, was a nexus of the counterculture and technologists. The catalog advocated "access to tools" as an avenue for sustainability and individual freedom, pushing readers to hack and tinker their way beyond the reach of "the Man."[5] The appearance of the catalog and the DIY mentality it advocated fed into a broader cultural attitude toward the computer as an impetus for peer-to-peer communication, nonhierarchical power structures, freedom of information, and personal

5  Stewart Brand, *The Updated Last Whole Earth Catalog: Access to Tools* (New York: Random House), 1974.

**P. SCOTT MAKELA AND
LAURIE HAYCOCK MAKELA**
Spread from *Whereishere*, 1998.
A collaboration with writer Lewis
Blackwell, *Whereishere* expressed the
multimedia frenzy spreading through
the design world in the 1990s. At the
time they were writing, the Makelas
were resident co-chairs of 2-D design
at Cranbrook Academy of Art.

6  See Fred Turner, *From Counter-culture to Cyberculture: Stewart Brand, the Whole Earth Network, and the Rise of Digital Utopianism* (Chicago: University of Chicago Press, 2006).

empowerment.[6] These concepts took on greater significance in the subsequent decades as they became embedded in the collaborative, open-source software development culture that started to influence the creative process of many graphic designers.

### RESISTING CENTRAL PROCESSING (1980-2000)

Once personal computers entered the creative arena in the mid-1980s, artists and designers could get their hands on real computers and interact with actual machines. The greater art and design scene began to embrace aesthetic complexity. Poststructuralist theories of openness and instability of meaning permeated graphic design, and the modernist focus on streamlined, objective forms wavered. New Wave in Los Angeles, the postmodern experiments led by Katherine McCoy and P. Scott and Laurie Haycock Makela at Cranbrook Academy of Art, and David Carson's work for *Ray Gun* magazine witnessed the objective, efficient forms of modernism give way to complex, layered aesthetics that asked users to determine the message for themselves. Graphic designers began to engage with technology to construct rich visual worlds through active exchanges with users.

The first Macintosh personal computer also ushered in the first mass-market laser printer: the HP LaserJet. Together these two tools of 1984 started to destabilize mass production and its corresponding design methodologies, which had emerged in the late 1800s and early 1900s, the decades following the Industrial Revolution, when mass production divorced design from manufacturing. The expense and therefore the risk of a project fell on the production stage under these conditions. For that reason designers pored over each precise detail of a project before releasing their ideas to professional

7  See Hugh Dubberly's discussion of manufacturing versus software development in "Design in the Age of Biology: Shifting from a Mechanical-Object Ethos to an Organic-Systems Ethos," *Interactions* 15, no. 5 (2008): 35-41.

printers and manufacturers.[7] The weighty expense of labor and materials pressured graphic forms into streamlined, efficient, standardized units. The early-twentieth-century mass-production model was thus determining both the typical design process and the resulting aesthetic. In the 1980s, however, designers such as Sharon Poggenpohl and Muriel Cooper recognized that emerging technologies could provide an escape from these restrictions.

As director of the Visual Language Workshop at the Massachusetts Institute of Technology (MIT), Cooper urged her students to hack and tinker with production equipment—at first offset printers, later photocopiers, laser printers, and computers. What happens, she wondered, when production is put back into the hands of the designer? What happens when communication is

8 Muriel Cooper, "Computers and Design," *Design Quarterly* 142 (1989): 4-31.

no longer "controlled, centralized" for distribution to mass audiences?[8] Cooper saw computers as a liberating force that would empower creatives to work more collaboratively and intuitively. Emerging technologies would free designers to iterate and test their work more easily, an integrated work style she considered more akin to the intuitive inquiries of the sciences. Cooper's ideas later flourished in the work of cultural theorists such as Yochai Benkler, Henry Jenkins, and Pierre Lévy.

Both inside and outside the professional design world, the desktop publishing industry thrived during this period. Despite fears of professional redundancy, many writers and designers reveled in their ability to put together layouts on the computer and then produce them on desktop printers. Rudy VanderLans and Zuzana Licko epitomized this movement with the launch

9 To read more about *Emigre,* see Rudy VanderLans and Zuzana Licko, *Emigre: Graphic Design into the Digital Realm* (New York: Van Nostrand Reinhold, 1993).

of Emigre Fonts and the popular magazine Emigre.[9] Licko designed typefaces directly on the Mac for immediate application by VanderLans in the latest issue of Emigre. For a long time designers had been restricted by expensive type foundries and typesetters, so the immediacy of computer-aided production captured the imagination of type designers, in particular.

A typographic renaissance resulted, including the creation of a bevy of radical digital typefaces as well as explorations of mutating form that built upon the algorithmic approaches of the 1960s. In 1989 Just van Rossum and Erik van Blokland, collaborating as LettError, began experimenting with "programming-assisted design" and released their RandomFont typeface Beowolf. Using radical postscript technology, they set parameters and then

10 Just van Rossum and Erik van Blokland, "Is Best Really Better," *Emigre* 18 (1990): n.p.

asked the computer to randomly vary those parameters.[10] Such experiments resulted in aesthetic form that had not been practical prior to the existence of personal computers. Complexity no longer equated with expense. Large production runs were no longer needed to justify setup costs. Laser printers joined with computation to make one-off forms economically feasible.

Many creatives took on the mantle of designer/programmer in the 1990s. These inquisitive souls believed that if software shaped their creative process and aesthetics, then to truly pursue their creative path, they had to build their own computational tools. John Maeda, director of the MIT Media Lab Aesthetics and Computation Group (ACG) from 1996 to 2003, inspired a generation of such designers/programmers, including Casey Reas, Ben Fry, Golan Levin, Peter Cho, and Reed Kram. In 1999 Maeda released his book Design by Numbers, in which he insists that computation is a unique medium, akin to pure thought, "because it is the only medium where the material and the process for shaping the material coexist in the same entity: numbers."[11]

11 John Maeda, *Design by Numbers* (Cambridge: MIT Press, 1999).

Maeda advocates for artists' and designers' direct engagement with raw computation and attempts through his Design by Numbers project to make the medium more accessible.

Inspired by Maeda's work, Casey Reas and Ben Fry went on to release Processing, an open-source language and environment, in 2001. Their language realizes the dream of a computing environment attainable by visual thinkers. Processing gave creatives access to a programming language, encouraging users to build their own tools and develop an aesthetics only possible through computation. Open-source development, which provides free access to the source code of computer programs, fed a large portion of the Processing project. Communities of artists and programmers pooled resources and knowledge to make the powerful tool freely available to all.[12] The project exemplifies a twenty-first-century shift in working style from individual and small team–based creative efforts to distributed, network-based projects in which unrelated individuals work together across time and space. Such efforts bring to fruition the egalitarian "Access to Tools" concept Brand propagated with the *Whole Earth Catalog* and other endeavors earlier in the century. The culture of software development was permeating the creative methods of the design world.[13]

## ENCODING THE FUTURE (2000 TO PRESENT)

In the early 1990s, the Internet spread beyond academia and into everyday people's lives. The personal computer morphed into a large networked mind through which creatives could think, make, collaborate, and distribute. Users commonly experienced content through active engagement online: pressing a button, scrolling down a page, uploading content, customizing interfaces. Interactivity took over.

The new millennium saw social media magnify the shareability of content. Designers built upon their discipline's understanding of systems thinking—which had been so popular in the 1960s—to create parameters for rich, welcoming environments. Such environments—whether a website, a digital publication, a game, or an app—scaffold user experience. Behavior trumps visually appealing fixed formats. As Khoi Vinh notes in "Conversations with the Network," "[I]n this new world designers are critical not so much for the transmission of message but for the crafting of the spaces within which those messages can be borne."[14] Monologues morph into conversations. Users actively participate in designs through a many-to-many communication model rather than passively receiving one-to-many broadcast messages.

12  By resisting traditional twentieth-century copyright, which prevents programmers from sharing resources, activist Richard Stallman's free software movement, founded in 1983, the copyleft movement, which began around the same period, and activist Lawrence Lessig's Creative Commons licenses made open-source development possible.

13  To learn more about how collaborative-making models influenced contemporary development models, see Eric S. Raymond, *The Cathedral and the Bazaar*, ed. Tim O'Reilly (Sebastopol, CA: O'Reilly & Associates, 1999).

14  Khoi Vinh, "Conversations with the Network," in *Talk to Me: Design and Communication Between People and Objects* (New York: Museum of Modern Art, 2011), 128-31.

Hugh Dubberly, co-creator of Apple's well-known technology-forecast film of 1987, *Knowledge Navigator*, asserts that we are moving from a "mechanical-object ethos" to an "organic-systems ethos." He points out that in contrast to the rigid mechanical brain of the last century, we now describe our computer networks in flexible biological terms, such as "bugs, viruses, attacks, communities, social capital, trust, identity." The modernist design methodology of the 1900s coalesced around reducing complex, chaotic information into simple, orderly forms by forcing materials and layouts into streamlined, efficient designs of our choosing. In the current century, Dubberly emphasizes, the massive increase in computer-processing power has enabled us to look instead to biology as a model for growing complex systems out of simple elements.[15]

Paola Antonelli, senior curator of art and design and director of research and development at the Museum of Modern Art (MoMA), considers biomimicry and nanotechnology to be natural steps in the move toward organic, systems-based work. She explains: "Nanotechnology, in particular, offers the promise of the principle of self-assembly and self-organization that one can find in cells, molecules, and galaxies; the idea that you would need only to give the components of an object a little push for the object to come together and reorganize in different configurations."[16] We are moving beyond twentieth-century systems thinking into a period in which we frame systems that can evolve on their own. This change in process— simple to complex rather than complex to simple—is only possible through the processing power of computation and the connectivity underpinned by the Internet.

Emergent behavior, a topic long discussed in computer science circles, has become a buzzword of the design disciplines. In the 2000s, creatives including Luna Maurer, Edo Paulus, Jonathan Puckey, and Roel Wouters of the collective Conditional Design expressed their desire to produce work appropriate to the now, exhibiting a passion akin to that of the avant-garde. They build upon the work of other generative designers, including Karsten Schmidt and Michael Schmitz, to delve purposefully into processes. Through a combination of rigorous process, logic, and organic input from "nature, society, and its human interactions," Conditional Design hopes to identify emergent patterns.[17] In such work, the ideology of John Conway's cellular automaton, the famous Game of Life, combines with algorithmic design thinking and making to physically and digitally produce artifacts of unexpected behavior.[18]

15 Hugh Dubberly, "Design in the Age of Biology: Shifting from a Mechanical-Object Ethos to an Organic-Systems Ethos" *Interactions* 15, no. 5 (2008), 35–41.

16 Paola Antonelli, "Design and the Elastic Mind," in *Design and the Elastic Mind* (New York: Museum of Modern Art, 2008), 19–24.

17 Luna Maurer, Edo Paulus, Jonathan Puckey, and Roel Wouters, "Conditional Design Manifesto," *Conditional Design*, April 3, 2015, http://conditionaldesign.org/manifesto.

18 British mathematician John Horton Conway developed the cellular automaton called Game of Life in 1970. Conway's game is often cited in discussions of emergence and self-organization.

The Internet of Things (IoT), also referred to as "ubiquitous" or "pervasive computing," currently inspires fresh design directions as well. We see inklings of a world beyond the screen as the objects around us slowly come to life through networks of embedded sensors. Virtual reality pioneer Brenda Laurel envisions ubiquitous computing as a way to become more closely connected to biosystems, deepening our knowledge so that we might behave more responsibly.[19] Embedding computation in the environment provides clear opportunities for engaging more fully with the human body and mind, thereby escaping from what developer Bret Victor sarcastically refers to as "pictures under glass."[20]

Futurists such as Hans Moravec and Ray Kurzweil see pervasive connectivity as a step in the evolution of transhuman intelligence: the technological singularity. Kurzweil predicts that around 2045 we will be forced to merge with intelligent machines—becoming a hybrid of biological and nonbiological intelligence—to keep up with the accelerating pace of change.[21] With such forecasts in mind, interaction experience designer Haakon Faste, in an essay written especially for this volume, urges designers to reexamine what it means to be human, and by doing so take a long, hard look at how our practice could affect this looming vision of a society predicated on intelligence beyond the bounds of biological evolution.

Biomimicry, nanotechnology, emergent behavior, ubiquitous computing, and the specter of the transhuman: this is the designer's current environment of practice. There is no going back. In the face of exponential technological growth, we have changed our process. We prototype, iterate, and respond instantly to user participation. Our methodology now mimics that of software developers as we release early and often. Influenced by open-source models of collaborative making and peer-to-peer production, we hack, think, make, and improve our discipline, a discipline vibrantly embedded within, rather than set apart from, everyday life. To quote Keetra Dean Dixon, designers today "walk the line between knowing and not knowing."[22] After all, isn't giving form to the yet-to-exist what designers do best?

The spelling and formatting of essay footnotes in this collection appear as they did in the original essays, except for some minor spelling changes for consistency. Please note that all original footnotes appear in black while additions by the author appear in red.

19 Brenda Laurel, "Designed Animism," in *(Re)Searching the Digital Bauhaus* (New York: Springer, 2009) 251-74.

20 Bret Victor, "A Brief Rant on the Future of Interaction Design," Worrydream.com, April 3, 2015, http://worrydream.com/#!/ABriefRantOnTheFutureOfInteractionDesign.

21 Ray Kurzweil, *The Singularity Is Near: When Humans Transcend Biology* (New York: Viking, 2005). Hans Moravec, "Robots, After All," *Communications of the ACM* 46, no. 10 (2003), 90-97.

22 Keetra Dean Dixon, "A Little Knowledge and Other Minor Daredeviling," (presentation, TYPO San Francisco, April 12, 2013).

1890 1900 1910 1920 1930 1940 1950

LADISLAV SUTNAR 1897-1976

BRUNO MUNARI 1907-1998

MAX BILL 1908-1994

MURIEL COOPER 1925-1994

WIM CROUWEL 1928-

SOL LEWITT 1928-2007

KARL GERSTNER 1930-

IVAN E. SUTHERLAND 1938-

STEWART BRAND 1938-

ALAN KAY 1940-

SHARON POGGENPOHL 1943-

APRIL GREIMAN 194

BRENDA LAURE

# TIMELINE

— LIFE SPAN OF EACH DESIGNER

● PUBLICATION DATE OF ANTHOLOGIZED TEXT

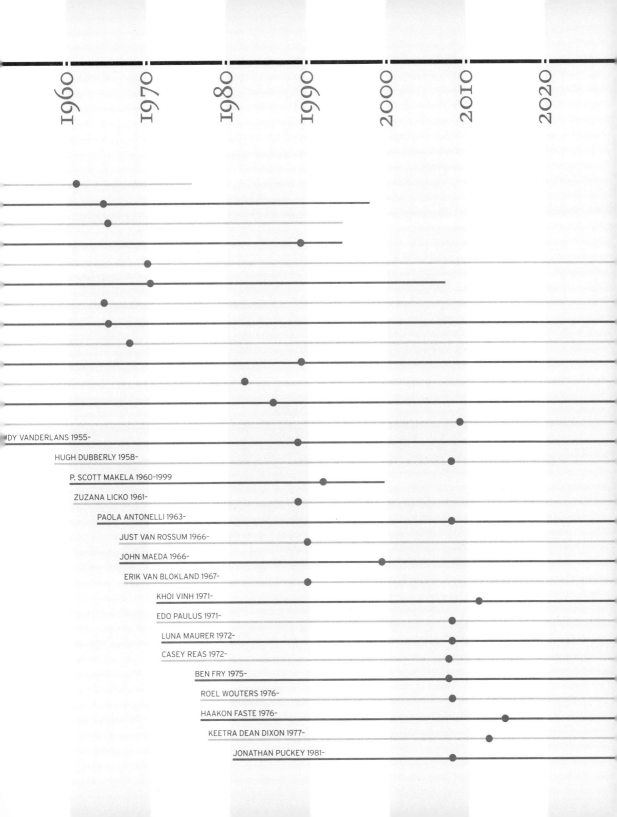

1960 1970 1980 1990 2000 2010 2020

DY VANDERLANS 1955–

HUGH DUBBERLY 1958–

P. SCOTT MAKELA 1960–1999

ZUZANA LICKO 1961–

PAOLA ANTONELLI 1963–

JUST VAN ROSSUM 1966–

JOHN MAEDA 1966–

ERIK VAN BLOKLAND 1967–

KHOI VINH 1971–

EDO PAULUS 1971–

LUNA MAURER 1972–

CASEY REAS 1972–

BEN FRY 1975–

ROEL WOUTERS 1976–

HAAKON FASTE 1976–

KEETRA DEAN DIXON 1977–

JONATHAN PUCKEY 1981–

# STRUCTURING THE DIGITAL

**DESIGNERS OF THE 1960S AND '70S DEVISED SYSTEMS FOR GRAPPLING WITH THE ACCELERATION OF MASS PRODUCTION, GLOBAL CONSUMERISM, AND THE RESULTING ONSLAUGHT OF DATA.** Influenced by the Bauhaus legacy and the subsequent development of Swiss style work, Ladislav Sutnar, Max Bill, and Karl Gerstner pursued precise, programmatic methodologies for effective design. Their projects answered postwar corporate appeals for visual unity, organized data, and universal communication. Mathematics is threaded through the projects of Bill and Gerstner, showing points of confluence, if only theoretically, with evolving mainframe computers. Mainframes loomed over these decades, first as elite, highly specialized machines and later as multipurpose, albeit prohibitively expensive, tools. Interest in computers arose among prescient artists, writers, scientists, and designers. Stewart Brand led a desktop publishing project—the *Whole Earth Catalog*—that empowered individuals to tinker and hack their way to an alternative, more sustainable lifestyle. The New Tendencies movement, centered in Zagreb, Croatia, organized exhibitions and conferences to probe the effect of computation on art and society. Conceptual artist Sol LeWitt looked beyond the finished product to define art as a field of possibilities. At the same time, designers and programmers such as Wim Crouwel and Ivan Sutherland explored interaction and aesthetics, particularly on early screens. Propelled by their love of systems, designers stretched out their hands to the computer and began to seize hold.

**MAINFRAME COMPUTER, CIRCA 1960**
IBM released its first general-use computer system, the System/360, in 1964.

**LADISLAV SUTNAR SOUGHT TO TAME THE CHAOTIC MASS OF TWENTIETH-CENTURY DATA WITH SIMPLICITY AND ORDER.** Like other postwar European designers, he turned away from decorative traditions, developing principles of functional design more appropriate to industrialized society. A Czech constructivist who mingled with Bauhaus masters, Sutnar transformed existing modernist principles into the early tenets of information design. He developed many of his systems-based innovations, such as the use of parentheses to designate U.S. area codes, after emigrating to the United States. In 1939 he traveled from Czechoslovakia to New York City to gather materials from the Czech pavilion at the World's Fair, and while he was abroad, Hitler invaded his home country. Sutnar remained in New York, forced to leave his wife and children in Prague. In addition to running his own agency in New York, he partnered with Knud Lönberg-Holm, director of information research for Sweet's Catalog Service, to reenvision catalog design.[1] Together they organized masses of information with grids, graphic icons, and tabbed systems, sharing their knowledge with the public in several books. Sutnar recognized that the advance of technology and the surge of the postwar economy demanded efficient communication. As he explains in the following essay from his seminal book of 1961, *Visual Design in Action*, "the watchword of today is 'faster, faster'–produce faster, distribute faster, communicate faster."

1  To learn more about Sutnar's immigration to the United States and his collaboration with Lönberg-Holm, read Steven Heller, "Sutnar & Lönberg-Holm: The Gilbert and Sullivan of Design," *Graphic Design Reader* (New York: Allworth, 2002), 177-85.

2  The format of this essay reflects Sutnar's original layout.

3  Title of book by W. J. Eckert and Rebecca Jones, 1955.

# VISUAL DESIGN IN ACTION

**LADISLAV SUTNAR | 1961**

**THE NEW TYPOGRAPHY'S EXPANDING FUTURE[2]**

**1—NEW NEEDS DEMAND NEW MEANS_____"FASTER, FASTER"[3]**

1/a _____ [mass production the basic cause]:—An understanding of the advances in graphic design and typography requires an examination of the causes that produced them. These advances, which have resulted in a new high in dynamic visual information design, have been especially rapid during the last thirty years. They derive from another aspect of our lives that has seen equally striking changes and growth over the same period. This aspect is the rapid developments in industrial techniques that we call mass production.

1/b _____ [mass communication the immediate cause]:—Mass production was not possible without mass distribution, which in turn was not possible without mass selling. Mass selling was impossible without improved forms, and new forms, of communication techniques in newspapers, magazines, radio, and television, and even in the product and its packaging. The changes in these basic elements in our lives have spread to other fields. The architect needs the graphic designer to contribute a system of visual direction and identification to modern schools, stores, and shopping centers. Educators are demanding visual aids. The jet plane pilot cannot read his instrument panel fast enough to survive without efficient typography.

1/c _____ [faster visual communication the need]:—New means had to come to meet the quickening tempo of industry. Graphic design was forced to develop higher standards of performance to speed up the transmission of information. Like the title of a book, appropriately enough on electronic computers, the watchword of today is "faster, faster"—produce faster, distribute faster, communicate faster.

## 2—REJECTION OF THE TRADITIONAL AS WELL AS "MODERNISTIC" _____ "MOST WORKS ARE MOST BEAUTIFUL WITHOUT ORNAMENT" [WALT WHITMAN][4]

4  Walt Whitman, *Leaves of Grass*, 1855.

2/a _____ [most approaches not functional]:—All of the conventional and other nonfunctional approaches prove inadequate when tested by industry's new need for a dynamic system of information design. They fail to meet the requirements for functional information flow so necessary for fast perception. These requirements are—/a/—to provide visual interest to gain attention and start the eye moving,—/b/—to simplify visual organization for speed in reading and understanding, and—/c/—to provide visual continuity for clarity in sequence.

2/b _____ [traditional approaches inadequate]:—Traditional approaches are based on arbitrary rules. The Aldus Manucius ideal is "an even, silverish gray of all printing, in title and text, or in ornament." But this is monotonous and uninviting. The formalistic rules of the renaissance period for arranging book titles on a middle axis produced static forces of an equilibrium of symmetry. This had to be rejected as too immobile. And the nineteenth century arrangements with fantastic typefaces have to be abandoned as irrational, and as false as the meaningless "gingerbread" of American architecture.

2/c _____ ["modernistic" approaches not constructive]:—"Modernistic" approaches are based on formulas solely concerned with the decorative. From a functional standpoint they represent nothing more than another aspect of chinoiserie because they are strictly arrangements for decorative effects. They cannot meet the new needs.—The formalistic, the sentimental, the fashionable, and the speculative are but short-lived vogues with superficial aims. They do not offer a constructive approach to the substance of the design task at hand.

## 3—BACKGROUND OF CONTEMPORARY DESIGN_____
### "BEAUTY IS THE PROMISE OF FUNCTION" [HORATIO GREENOUGH]

3/a _____ [the "new typography"]:—A sound basis exists for modern graphic design and typography. It is a direct heritage of the avant-garde pioneering of the twenties and thirties in Europe. It represents a basic change that is revolutionary. This movement was first called "constructivistic," meaning constructed or having a logical structure, as opposed to the improvised or guided-by-personal-feelings. It was also called "functional typography" to emphasize the idea of a design planned to perform a function as contrasted to the use of formalistic rules, or art for art's sake. Later, the clear departure from the apathy of commercial tradition and from obsolete cliche became known as the "new typography." This name still stands for vigor of imaginative experiments, for innovations, and for the invention of new techniques. It reveals new potentials in visual communications.

3/b _____ [basis of "new typography"]:—As a sort of credo, in 1929 [Karel] Teige[5] characterized this new typography as follows:—/1/—freedom from tradition;—/2/—geometrical simplicity;—/3/—contrast of typographic material;—/4/—exclusion of any typographic ornament not functionally necessary;—/5/—preference for photography, for machine set type, and for combinations of primary colors; finally: recognition and acceptance of the machine age and the utilitarian purpose of typography. These points were quoted by [Jan] Tschichold as a framework of his book *Eine Stunde Druckgestaltung* [A Lesson in Creative Typographical Design].

3/c _____ [the social implications of the "new typography"]:—In 1934, in a talk at the opening of an exhibition of Sutnar's graphic work, Teige attempted to formulate the new social function of the graphic designer and his relation to his environment. Freely translated, he said:—/1/—our world is the world of today, on the march to tomorrow's—/2/—our service is that of a public servant in its best sense, aimed at progressive development of higher cultural standards;—/3/—our work is that of graphic editor, graphic architect, graphic planner—understanding and employing advanced methods of mechanized printing, collaborating with the expert in the printing plant. He also observed that as an exception, some visual poems [montage-typography] may resemble the work of poets. That, where done for utilitarian reasons, the modern typographer's work can be compared in "the categories of arts in transition" with journalism and with the work of the architect-planner in the way of thinking and approach.[6]

5 Karel Teige, writer and editor of magazines and books on modern architecture and art.

6 "Sutnar and New Typography," Teige; *Panorama Magazine*, Prague, January 1934.

## 4—PRINCIPLES OF CONTEMPORARY INFORMATION DESIGN_____
_____"DESIGN IS A PROCESS OF STRUCTURAL DEFINITION"
## [K. LÖNBERG-HOLM]

4/a _____ [fundamental design principles necessary]:—In his book Vision in Motion [1947] [Lázló] Moholy-Nagy devotes an entire chapter to discussing the idea that "designing is not a profession but an attitude." In recent years sincere efforts in espousing the original meaning of the new typography, with its endeavor to create lasting values, have been hampered by blurred imitations. Advertising stunts have ridiculed the moral forces behind the movement. Even so, progressive evolution of the new typography could not be stopped. An occasional look back to its real origins is necessary to avoid some present day misconceptions. Bolstered by this knowledge and with present day experience, principles of sound design for universal application can be stated.

4/b _____ [fundamental design principles defined]:—Depending on the requirements of specific problem needs, the varied aspects of design can be reduced to three interacting, fundamental principles—function, flow, and form. These may be defined as follows:—"Function" is the quality that satisfies utilitarian needs by meeting a specific purpose or goal.—"Flow" is the quality that satisfies logical needs by providing a space-time sequence relationship of elements.—"Form" is the quality that satisfies aesthetic needs with respect to the basic elements of size, blank space, color, line, and shape.[7]

7 "Catalog Design Progress," Lönberg-Holm and Sutnar, 1950.

4/c _____ [new design synthesis]:—With these three principles as a basis, design is evaluated as a process culminating in an entity that intensifies comprehension. The design aspects could be analytically polarized further into function vs. form, utility vs. beauty, rational vs. irrational. The function of design in this regard is established as one of resolving the conflict of these polarities into a new design synthesis.

## 5—THE NEW TYPOGRAPHY IN USA_____"PROGRESS IS
## OUR MOST IMPORTANT PRODUCT" [GENERAL ELECTRIC][8]

8 Advertising slogan.

5/a ___ [the "new typography" has taken root]:—Anyone visiting this country for the first time cannot avoid being surprised by the multitude of printed matter and by the diversity of attitudes toward graphic design and typography. Here, now, is an internationally recognized "l'ecole de New York" in pioneering abstract art. It rivals the older "l'ecole de Paris" by the unquestionable merit of its achievements. Here, also, is a rapidly growing school of "new typography USA," inspired by Europe's early example and representing a wealth of new findings in visual communications.

**LADISLAV SUTNAR**
*Visual Design in Action*
**1961**

9 *This Week Magazine,*
August 7, 1960.

5/b _____ [solutions not found in history]:—It is difficult today to visualize any effect that [Leonardo] da Vinci's vision of a flying man can have on modern research in aviation. It is equally difficult to see how the "traditional" or "liberal conservative" should be allowed to influence further development of the new typography in the United States. Even in the field of book design, only emotional prejudice, inertia, and conventionalism obstruct design advances. A book's structural form has not varied for centuries. Even so, the dynamism of new design standards and the principles of contemporary design are finding their way into this field. There is just one lesson from the past that should be learned for the benefit of the present. It is that of the painstaking, refined craftsmanship that appears to be dying out.

5/c _____ [opportunity for innovation is unique]:—The spectacular complexity and variety of printed communications in this country offers the American designer unparalleled opportunities. Magazines with hundreds of pages, catalogs with thousands of pages, all with their implications of enormous advertising expenditures, are unique to this country. This wealth of work also brings extensive means of reproduction. The larger the opportunity the greater is the danger of opportunism and hesitancy in accepting innovations. But there is no other way to sound design solutions than by open-minded and educated thinking. This means intensive study and analysis of the needs and extensive research in the design and production means to meet these needs.

**6—FUTURE ADVANCES IN GRAPHIC DESIGN_____**
**"TOMORROW IS MADE UP OF THE SUM TOTAL OF TODAY'S EXPERIENCES"**
**[(BORIS) PASTERNAK][9]**

6/a _____ [need is evident and urgent]:—With the world becoming ever smaller, a new sense of world interdependence comes sharply into focus. And with it a new need for visual information capable of worldwide comprehension becomes evident. This will require many new types of visual information, simplified information systems, and improved forms and techniques. It will also make urgent the development of mechanical devices for information processing, integration, and transmission. These advances will also have their influence on the design of visual information for domestic consumption.

6/b _____ [faster progress after agreement on principles]:—The way to the advances of tomorrow requires agreement on and ever widening use of basic principles. This is the way accelerated progress came in the natural sciences.—

Euclid's axioms in geometry, Newton's laws, and Einstein's theories in physics, to name but a few.—When these come to graphic design, then the smart gimmicks, the short-lived effects of contradictory modes, the emotional style revivals, the speculative new false styles, the novelties of typeface preference, and the assorted variety of "safe" formulas for sure results, all will be quickly forgotten.

6/c _____ [progress will be in proportion to our integrity]:—We have readily accepted the rapid tempo of advances in science and technology where the inventions of yesterday are today's realities. Similarly, the potential advances of today's new graphic design are building a knowledge of design vocabulary that will be taken for granted tomorrow. And the creative forces at work will find their basic validity in terms of the human values of sincerity, honesty, and the belief in the meaningfulness of one's work, in people who disregard material advantages for the sake of new experiments that will make future developments possible.

**LADISLAV SUTNAR** Spreads from *Design and Paper: Number 13, Controlled Visual Flow*, 1943. Sutnar was one of the earliest designers to envision facing pages as spreads.

**BRUNO MUNARI REJECTED EXCLUSIVITY IN FAVOR OF ART AND DESIGN THAT CONNECTED AND SERVED. HIS PROJECTS ACTIVATED VIEWERS, ASKING THEM TO PARTICIPATE IN THE WORK BEFORE THEM.** He engaged with the public as a painter, sculptor, graphic artist, industrial designer, and author. In the early part of the twentieth century Munari was a member of Filippo Tommaso Marinetti's futurist group, but he distanced himself from the movement after World War II when its fascist sympathies began to emerge. In 1948 he helped found the Italian concrete art movement. His interest in projects that were open to viewer interaction led to his involvement with the New Tendencies movement. Inspired by 1960s mainframe computers, this group of designers, artists, engineers, mathematicians, and scientists strived to develop a technological aesthetics that bridged art and science. Disgusted by the faddish consumer nature of the gallery scene, they saw computers as the key medium for a more useful twentieth-century visual culture.[1] In 1962 Munari organized an influential exhibition that showcased the early figures of the New Tendencies movement. Sponsored by the Olivetti Company, *Arte programmata. Arte cinetica. Opera moltiplicate. Opera aperta.* (Programmed Art. Kinetic Art. Multiplied Works. Open Works.), was held first in Olivetti's Italian and German showrooms and later shown in the United States. The projects challenged the viewers' sense of perception. Some pieces shifted visually as viewers moved, for example, suggesting a kinetic quality. The "programmed" aspect was not algorithmic in a contemporary sense, as Umberto Eco explained in the accompanying catalog, but rather "a formative practice...according to a dialectic of planning and randomness." In his introduction Eco praised the "dynamic of perception" expressed in *Arte programmata*: "Aesthetic pleasure was no longer—or at least not always—derived from looking at complete and fully achieved organisms, but rather from seeing organisms in an indefinite process of completion."[2] The concept of "programmed" work, brought to the forefront by Munari's exhibition, permeated the New Tendencies movement in the years to follow, taking on a variety of connotations as artists and designers sought to understand the potential of computers and visual research.

1 To read more about the New Tendencies movement, see Margit Rosen, *A Little-Known Story About a Movement, a Magazine, and the Computer's Arrival in Art: New Tendencies and Bit International, 1961-1973* (Cambridge: MIT Press, 2011).

2 Umberto Eco, introduction, *Arte programmata. Arte cinetica. Opera moltiplicate. Opera aperta.* (Milan: Olivetti, 1962).

# ARTE PROGRAMMATA

**BRUNO MUNARI | 1964**

We are all familiar with the traditional methods and techniques by which artists have given substance to their fancies in all epochs. We know that images in two or three dimensions (pictures and sculptures) are obtained by these means, and we know also that these images are subjective, static, unique, and definitive. This is true whether they are reproductions of visible nature, personal interpretations, impressions, stylizations, deformations of visible nature, or even invented relationships and chromatic, formal, and volumetric harmonies, as in the case of abstract art.

We know too that art is always the same even if the methods and techniques of setting it forth change, that changing the means does not change the art, that art is not a method and method is not art. One might say in fact that every creative intuition has, in the absolute sense, its ideal means, more suitable than any other for revealing itself, and that not all visual art must perforce be painting or sculpture.

As times change, man's sensibilities change with them. A static image, unique and final, does not contain that quantity of information sufficient to interest the contemporary viewer, who is accustomed to live in an environment subject to simultaneous and multifarious stimuli from the most varied sources.

This situation gives birth to programmed art, which has as its ultimate aim the production not of a single definitive and subjective image, but of a multitude of images in continual variation. The "programming" of these works, which necessarily, because of technical reasons and limitations, are neither paintings nor sculptures, is to be understood in the sense that each artist chooses a particular material and the structural, kinetic, and optical combinations that he considers most suitable for the embodiment of his artistic intuition. Consequently, in keeping with the rules of "good design" (in the same way as a fish has the form of a fish and a rose the form and substance of a rose) the object he makes will have its most natural form.

In these works of programmed art the fundamental elements, which, along with the kinetic and optical combinations, will give life to a continuous series of images, are in a free state or are arranged objectively in geometrically ordered systems so as to create the greatest number of combinations, often unpredictable in their mutations but all programmed in accordance with the system planned by the artist.

A work of programmed art is thus to be observed and considered not as an object representing something else, but as "the thing" in itself to be observed. It is a field of events, an area of a previously unknown world of creativity, a fragment of a new reality to be observed in its continual variations.

**KARL GERSTNER MAPPED THE DESIGN PROCESS INTO AN "ORGANIZED INVENTORY OF POSSIBILITIES," RECOGNIZING THE POTENTIAL IMPACT OF COMPUTATION UPON GRAPHIC DESIGN.**[1] He followed intellectually on the heels of Max Bill and Paul Lohse, applying Swiss style concepts at his successful agency Gerstner + Kutter in Basel, Switzerland—founded in 1959 with public relations specialist Markus Kutter—while exploring concrete art in his personal work. He thrived on the intensity of agency life, working for clients such as Geigy, IBM, and Ford. In 1964, the same year that IBM announced its popular mainframe computer System/360, Gerstner wrote *Designing Programmes: Instead of Solutions for Problems, Programmes for Solutions.* In 1974 he published *Compendium for Literates: A System of Writing.* Both books use astrophysicist Fritz Zwicky's morphological method to construct a systematic approach that catalogs all possible variables. As Gerstner explains, "The process of designing is reduced to an act of selection: crossing and linking parameters."[2] The simplicity and order of Swiss style typography, the mathematical precision of concrete art, and an understanding of procedural literacy—Gerstner drew on all these ideas just as mainframe computing began to permeate the larger creative culture.

1  Blurb on the dust jacket of the first edition of Karl Gerstner, *Compendium for Literates: A System of Writing* (Cambridge: MIT Press, 1974).

2. Quoted by Manfred Kroplien in his foreword to Karl Gerstner, *Review of 5x10 Years of Graphic Design etc.* (Ostfildern-Ruit, Germany: Hatje Cantz, 2001).

a  Basis

| 1. Components | 11. Word | 12. Abbreviation | 13. Word group | 14. Combined | |
|---|---|---|---|---|---|
| 2. Typeface | 21. Sans-serif | 22. Roman | 23. German | 24. Some other | 25. Combined |
| 3. Technique | 31. Written | 32. Drawn | 33. Composed | 34. Some other | 35. Combined |

b  Colour

| 1. Shade | 11. Light | 12. Medium | 13. Dark | 14. Combined | |
|---|---|---|---|---|---|
| 2. Value | 21. Chromatic | 22. Achromatic | 23. Mixed | 24. Combined | |

c  Appearance

| 1. Size | 11. Small | 12. Medium | 13. Large | 14. Combined | |
|---|---|---|---|---|---|
| 2. Proportion | 21. Narrow | 22. Usual | 23. Broad | 24. Combined | |
| 3. Boldness | 31. Lean | 32. Normal | 33. Fat | 34. Combined | |
| 4. Inclination | 41. Upright | 42. Oblique | 43. Combined | | |

**MORPHOLOGICAL BOX** Diagram accompanying "Programme as Logic" in Gerstner's *Designing Programmes.* As he explains, "It contains the criteria—the parameters on the left, the relative components on the right—following which marks and signs are to be designed from letters. The criteria are rough. As the work proceeds, of course, they are to be refined as desired."

d  Expression

| 1. Reading direction | 11. From left to right | 12. From top to bottom | 13. From bottom to top | 14. Otherwise | 15. Combined |
|---|---|---|---|---|---|
| 2. Spacing | 21. Narrow | 22. Normal | 23. Wide | 24. Combined | |
| 3. Form | 31. Unmodified | 32. Mutilated | 33. Projected | 34. Something else | 35. Combined |
| 4. Design | 41. Unmodified | 42. Something omitted | 43. Something replaced | 44. Something added | 45. Combined |

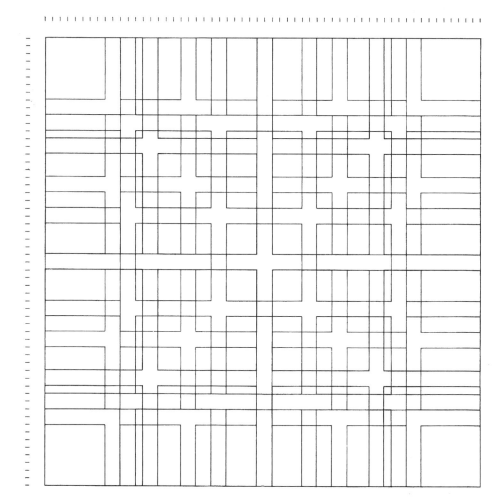

# DESIGNING PROGRAMMES

**KARL GERSTNER | 1964**

### PROGRAM AS GRID

Is the grid a program? Let me put it more specifically: if the grid is considered as a proportional regulator, a system, it is a program par excellence. Squared paper is an (arithmetic) grid, but not a program. Unlike, say, the (geometric) module of Le Corbusier, that can, of course, be used as a grid but is primarily a program. Albert Einstein said of the module: "It is a scale of proportions that makes the bad difficult and the good easy." That is a programmatic statement of what I take to be the aim of *Designing Programmes*.

The typographic grid is a proportional regulator for composition, tables, pictures, etc. It is a formal program to accommodate x unknown items. The difficulty is: to find the balance, the maximum of conformity to a rule with the maximum of freedom. Or: the maximum of constants with the greatest possible variability.

In our agency we have evolved the "mobile grid." An example is the arrangement on the previous page: the grid for the periodical *Capital*.

The basic unit is ten points; the size of the basic typeface including the lead. The text and picture area are divided at the same time into one, two, three, four, five, and six columns. There are 58 units along the whole width. This number is a logical one when there are always two units between the columns. That is: it divides in every case without a remainder: with two columns the 58 units are composed of 2 x 28 + 2 (space between columns); with 3 columns 3 x 18 + 2 x 2; with 4 columns 4 x 13 + 3 x 2; with 5 columns 5 x 10 + 4 x 2; with 6 columns 6 x 8 + 5 x 2 10-point units.

The grid looks complicated to anyone not knowing the key. For the initiate it is easy to use and (almost) inexhaustible as a program.

## PROGRAM AS COMPUTER GRAPHICS

The illustrations [on the right] show pictures from the series 201. They came into being in 1966 and are the work of Frieder Nake, who is per se a programmer at the computing center of the Stuttgart Institute of Technology.

He writes: "Visual objects generated by computers and drawn by automatic drawing machines are solutions of aesthetic programs that are written by human beings and implemented by machines.

1. In a (more or less subjective) selection process, a person decides on a certain class of visual objects. In concrete terms this means: the elements that are fixed are to appear in the picture or pictures. In the examples below: horizontal or vertical lines of equal length.

2. He or others then formalize the problem radically so that it is suitable for the programming of an automatic production process in which man is involved simply in an ancillary and not a decisive capacity. This means that all the concepts arising (color, form, completion, selection, proximity, relation, tension, frequency, etc.) must be translated into mathematical language. When the problem has been formulated in mathematical terms, it is translated into a text that the computer can understand.

THE ACT OF DESCRIBING THE TASK IS PART OF THE SOLUTION....THE MORE PRECISE AND COMPLETE THESE CRITERIA ARE, THE MORE CREATIVE THE WORK.

KARL GERSTNER
*Review of 5x10*
*Years of Graphic*
*Design etc.*
2001

This translation is the "programming of a computer." For this purpose a "programming language" is used, e.g., ALGOL 60. In this language we find sentences like:

«for» i: = t «step» 1 «until» n «do»

«begin» x: = choose(mx, x1, x2); y: = choose(my, y1, y2)

Z: =choose (mz, z1, z2); zeichne {x, y, z}.

3. The program is delivered and passed onto modern computers that, working in conjunction with drawing machines, ensure that the process is carried out automatically and deliver the finished visual object. The use of chance generators plays an important part in this process since they simulate imagination, variations, and series formation. A program can be repeated virtually as often as desired without the same result ever occurring twice." F. N. [Frieder Nake]

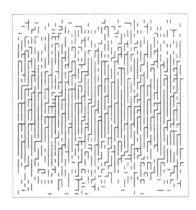

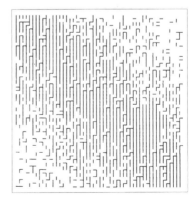

## PROGRAM AS MOVEMENT

"All elements of the visual are periodic, i.e., capable of being programmed at will." I was glad to have an opportunity to write a commentary on this theme. The opportunity was offered by the periodical *Graphic Design*, from which the following extracts are taken. I am, however, replacing the expression "periodic" by "continuous"; it is more apposite and precise.

Numbers are continuous: 1–2–3–4–5–6–7–8–9–10…The step between 1 and 2 is precisely the same size as that between 9 and 10. The steps can be refined ad lib.: 1–1.1–1.2…2 without the step between 1 and 2 being altered. This truism about numbers is also true of colors: colors are of their nature continuous. A series from white to black, e.g., in ten steps, each step the same size as the next and the one preceding it. Here the question is not one of counting but one of measuring. What is measured is the distance between two points. Between white and black there may be ten steps, or two, or two hundred (the human eye cannot distinguish more): a certain gray will always occupy the same place, an exactly intermediate shade of gray will occupy a place exactly in the center between black and white, and so forth.

But not only white will pass over continuously into black but any color into any other color. Colors form a closed system. But not only colors but all the elements of the visual are continuous. Any form can pass over into any other. Any form of movement (a bird's flight for example) is a process of continuously changing forms, only in this case the change is "fluid." It is because any movement can be resolved back into single forms = phases that the film is possible: it consists of twenty-four static but continuous single pictures that, when projected, again create the illusion of movement.

I am indebted to Mitsuo Katsui, Tokyo, for an example of a continuous change in the field of elementary geometry: he caused a triangle to merge "imperceptibly" into a circle.

THE *COMPENDIUM*…SUPPLIES PARAMETERS FOR THE PROGRAMMING OF AN ELECTRONICALLY CONTROLLED TYPE, THAT OF COMPUTERS, FOR A NOT-TOO-DISTANT FUTURE.

KARL GERSTNER
*Compendium
for Literates*
1974

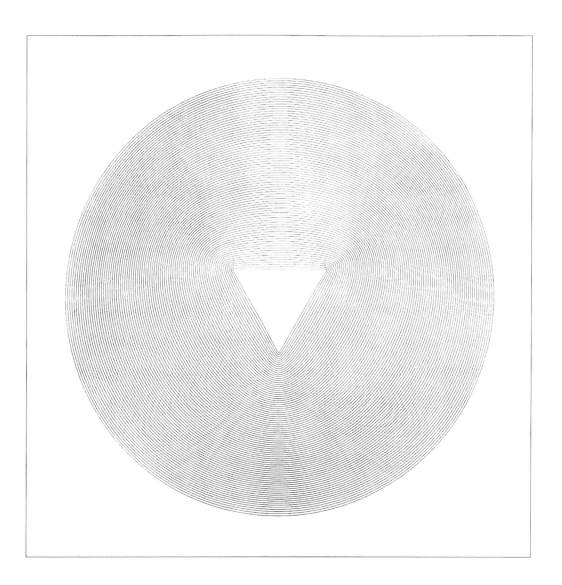

**IN 1963 IVAN SUTHERLAND CHANGED THE RELATIONSHIP BETWEEN HUMAN AND COMPUTER.**
While an electrical engineering doctoral student at MIT, he developed Sketchpad, the first computer program
to use a graphical user interface (GUI). Human-computer interaction was born. As Sutherland explained,
"The Sketchpad system makes it possible for a man and a computer to converse rapidly through the medium
of line drawings....In the past, we have been writing letters to rather than conferring with our computers."[1]
Sutherland used a light-sensitive pen to draw directly on the nine-inch display screen of the TX-2 computer
then found at MIT's Lincoln Laboratory. He realized that the resulting strokes could be manipulated on
the screen using set rules, locked into a single image, moved around, copied to build more complex images,
and even stored in a library to be used later. And all of this could happen in real time, facilitated by a general
user without programming expertise. Through Sketchpad, Sutherland threw open the doors of the computing
castle to engineers and designers. He made a short film of his discovery, *Sketchpad: A Man-Machine Graphical Communication System*, which became a cult classic in computer research circles.[2] Computer-aided design
(CAD) programs and object-oriented programming sprang from the ideas he introduced.

1. Ivan E. Sutherland, "Sketchpad: A Man-Machine Graphical Communication System," *AFIPS Conference Proceedings* 23 (1963): 8.

2. A digital copy of the 16mm film can be found on YouTube.

# THE ULTIMATE DISPLAY

## IVAN E. SUTHERLAND | 1965

We live in a physical world whose properties we have come to know well
through long familiarity. We sense an involvement with this physical world
that gives us the ability to predict its properties well. For example, we can
predict where objects will fall, how well-known shapes look from other
angles, and how much force is required to push objects against friction. We
lack corresponding familiarity with the forces on charged particles, forces in
nonuniform fields, the effects of nonprojective geometric transformations,
and high-inertia, low-friction motion. A display connected to a digital computer gives us a chance to gain familiarity with concepts not realizable in the
physical world. It is a looking glass into a mathematical wonderland.

Computer displays today cover a variety of capabilities. Some have only
the fundamental ability to plot dots. Displays being sold now generally have
built in line-drawing capability. An ability to draw simple curves would be
useful. Some available displays are able to plot very short line segments in
arbitrary directions, to form characters or more complex curves. Each of these
abilities has a history and a known utility.

3. K. C. Knowlton, "A Computer Technique for Producing Ani-mated Movies," in *Proceedings of the Spring Joint Computer Conference* (Washington, DC: Spartan, 1964).

It is equally possible for a computer to construct a picture made up of
colored areas. Knowlton's movie language, BEFLIX, is an excellent example of
how computers can produce area-filling pictures.[3] No display available com-
mercially today has the ability to present such area-filling pictures for direct

human use. It is likely that new display equipment will have area-filling capability. We have much to learn about how to make good use of this new ability.

The most common direct computer input today is the typewriter keyboard. Typewriters are inexpensive, reliable, and produce easily transmitted signals. As more and more online systems are used, it is likely that many more typewriter consoles will come into use. Tomorrow's computer user will interact with a computer through a typewriter. He ought to know how to touch type.

A variety of other manual-input devices are possible. The light pen or RAND Tablet stylus serves a very useful function in pointing to displayed items and in drawing or printing input to the computer. The possibilities for very smooth interaction with the computer through these devices is only just beginning to be exploited. RAND Corporation has in operation today a debugging tool that recognizes printed changes of register contents, and simple pointing and moving motions for format relocation. Using RAND's techniques, you can change a digit printed on the screen by merely writing what you want on top of it. If you want to move the contents of one displayed register into another, merely point to the first and "drag" it over to the second. The facility with which such an interaction system lets its user interact with the computer is remarkable.

Knobs and joysticks of various kinds serve a useful function in adjusting the parameters of some computation going on. For example, adjustment of the viewing angle of a perspective view is conveniently handled through a three-rotation joystick. Push buttons with lights are often useful. Syllable voice input should not be ignored.

In many cases the computer program needs to know which part of a picture the man is pointing at. The two-dimensional nature of pictures makes it impossible to order the parts of a picture by neighborhood. Converting from display coordinates to find the object pointed at is, therefore, a time-consuming process. A light pen can interrupt at the time that the display circuits transfer the item being pointed at, thus automatically indicating its address and coordinates. Special circuits on the RAND Tablet or other position input device can make it serve the same function.

What the program actually needs to know is where in memory is the structure that the man is pointing to. In a display with its own memory, a light pen return tells where in the display file the thing pointed to is, but not necessarily where in main memory. Worse yet, the program really needs to know which sub part of which part the man is pointing to. No existing display equipment computes the depths of recursions that are needed. New displays with analog memories may well lose the pointing ability altogether.

THE SKETCHPAD SYSTEM, BY ELIMINATING TYPED STATEMENTS (EXCEPT FOR LEGENDS) IN FAVOR OF LINE DRAWINGS, OPENS UP A NEW AREA OF MAN-MACHINE COMMUNICATION.

IVAN SUTHERLAND
"Sketchpad: A
Man-Machine Graphical
Communication System"
1963

## OTHER TYPES OF DISPLAY

If the task of the display is to serve as a looking glass into the mathematical wonderland constructed in computer memory, it should serve as many senses as possible. So far as I know, no one seriously proposes computer displays of smell, or taste. Excellent audio displays exist, but unfortunately we have little ability to have the computer produce meaningful sounds. I want to describe for you a kinesthetic display.

The force required to move a joystick could be computer controlled, just as the actuation force on the controls of a Link Trainer are changed to give the feel of a real airplane. With such a display, a computer model of particles in an electric field could combine manual control of the position of a moving charge, replete with the sensation of forces on the charge, with visual presentation of the charge's position.... By use of such an input/output device, we can add a force display to our sight and sound capability.

The computer can easily sense the positions of almost any of our body muscles. So far only the muscles of the hands and arms have been used for computer control. There is no reason why these should be the only ones, although our dexterity with them is so high that they are a natural choice. Our eye dexterity is very high also. Machines to sense and interpret eye motion data can and will be built. It remains to be seen if we can use a language of glances to control a computer. An interesting experiment will be to make the display presentation depend on where we look.

For instance, imagine a triangle so built that whichever corner of it you look at becomes rounded. What would such a triangle look like? Such experiments will lead not only to new methods of controlling machines, but also to interesting understandings of the mechanisms of vision.

There is no reason why the objects displayed by a computer have to follow the ordinary rules of physical reality with which we are familiar. The kinesthetic display might be used to simulate the motions of a negative mass. The user of one of today's visual displays can easily make solid objects transparent—he can "see through matter!" Concepts that never before had any visual representation can be shown, for example the "constraints" in Sketchpad.[4] By working with such displays of mathematical phenomena we can learn to know them as well as we know our own natural world. Such knowledge is the major promise of computer displays.

The ultimate display would, of course, be a room within which the computer can control the existence of matter. A chair displayed in such a room would be good enough to sit in. Handcuffs displayed in such a room would be confining, and a bullet displayed in such a room would be fatal. With appropriate programming such a display could literally be the Wonderland into which Alice walked.

4  Sutherland, "Sketchpad:
A Man-Machine Graphical
Communication System," in
Proceedings of the Spring
Joint Computer Conference
(Washington, DC: Spartan,
1964).

**MAX BILL BRIDGED THE GAP BETWEEN ART AND MATHEMATICS, INTUITION AND ORDER.**
Known for his pioneering role in the field of concrete art, the Swiss artist also established himself in commercial design through his publications, advertising work, exhibitions, and products. His approach to design was to establish a system of rules and then develop permutations of form that spring from those constraints. Mathematical formulas played a key role. This methodical, precise approach prefigured the work of twenty-first-century generative designers. Bill's approach demonstrates that before algorithms became a common theme, artists and designers were already exploring strict rule-based methodologies. Bauhaus ideals of functionality and simplicity permeate his work, although Bill himself attended the influential school for only two years. He left without a degree in 1929 to return to Zurich, open his own office, and practice both fine art and commercial work. As an industrial designer, Bill scoffed at forms driven by commercial profit, championing instead *die gute Form*. Such "honest forms," he believed, emerged in response to human need rather than passing trends of style, an opinion communicated to the larger culture in his influential 1952 book *Form*.[1] In the text that follows, Bill asserts a core principle of his practice, that "art can originate only when and because individual expression and personal invention subsume themselves under the principle of order."

1 Max Bill, *Form* (Basel: Karl Werner, 1952), 7–11.

# STRUCTURE AS ART? ART AS STRUCTURE?

**MAX BILL | 1965**

One can consider art to be essentially identifiable as invention. The invention of means of expression; the first thrust into realms that contain as yet unknown aesthetic and formal possibilities.

That is the sense in which art presupposes something novel. The newness of the idea, newness of the themes, newness of the form. This kind of newness can be achieved in two ways: (a) in an individual way—that has its origin in the intellectual and psychological makeup of the artist; (b) in a more general way—that bases itself on experimenting with objective possibilities of form. In an extreme case (a) will lead to "art informel" or to a neo-Dadaistic combination of materials; (b) leads to structure. On the one hand: materials in their "natural" condition, individually interpreted. On the other: tectonic laws that ultimately are schematically applied in a uniform distribution.

Even though amorphous material can be considered to possess an inner configuration—a structure of its own—in its natural condition, we can eliminate this kind of structure from our consideration, for as an inherent structure it is not accessible to aesthetic or visual arguments, either in painting or in sculpture.

THOUGHT IS ONE OF THE MOST ESSENTIAL CHARACTERISTICS OF MAN. THOUGHT MAKES IT POSSIBLE TO GIVE ORDER TO EMOTIONAL VALUE IN SUCH A WAY THAT WORKS OF ART CAN BE CREATED FROM IT.

MAX BILL
"Die mathematische
Denkweise in der
Kunst unserer Zeit"
1949

Tectonic laws are altogether different. They are accessible to aesthetic arguments for they are principally laws of order, and in the end art = order. In other words, art is neither a surrogate for nature, nor for individuality, nor for spontaneity. And where it appears as such, it is art only insofar as it informs the surrogate with order and form. Because order is so characteristic of art, art begins to rely for order on the tectonic laws.

Now the question arises as to what a tectonic law, a law of order, as we know it in science, means with respect to art. That is, where does structure end and art begin?

Let us start with the extreme case: a plane is covered with a uniform distribution in the sense in which this is understood in statistics; or a uniform network extends into space. This is an order that could be uniformly extended without end. Such an order we here call a structure. In a work of art, however, this structure has its limits, either in space or on the plane. Here we have the basis for an aesthetic argument in the sense that a choice has to be made: the possible, aesthetically feasible extension of the structure. Actually it is only through this choice to limit the arbitrarily extensible structure on the basis of verifiable arguments that a discernible principle of order becomes comprehensible.

But is a choice, or the setting of limits, sufficient for the creation of a work of art? This question arises mainly because, since the radical attempt to dispense with all individualistic stylistic expression beginning with [Piet] Mondrian, no reduction can be extreme enough. This also arises because the aesthetic information offered by the means of expression is dwindling sharply: *neither locatable nor measurable, neither expressing nor indicating an order*: producing a neuter with aesthetic pretensions. The aesthetic quality is beginning to withdraw into the most extreme reductions, into the most extreme objectivity, culminating ultimately in the negation of newness and of invention.

But invention always presupposes the discovery of new problems. The discovery of these new problems is individually determined. Art is unthinkable without the effort of the individual. Order on the other hand is impossible without an objectifying structure.

This means that art can originate only when and because individual expression and personal invention subsume themselves under the principle of order of the structure and derive from it a new lawfulness and new formal possibilities.

Such lawfulness and such inventions manifest themselves as rhythm in an individual case. Rhythm transforms the structure into form; i.e., the special form of a work of art grows out of the general structure by means of a rhythmic order.

**STEWART BRAND ALIGNED HIPPIE PASSION WITH TECHNOLOGICAL INNOVATION.** After studying biology, design, and photography, he joined with friends in 1968 to produce the *Whole Earth Catalog*, a compendium of tools and techniques. Brand committed to providing knowledge to amateurs, so that they might develop a positive, sustainable society through direct participation. This knowledge, Brand understood, included the liberating potential of the computer.[1] The same year as the release of the *Whole Earth Catalog*, Brand assisted in Douglas Engelbart's "Mother of All Demos," in which Engelbart revealed astonishing advances in the use of computers that still define our workday: the mouse, hypertext, word processing, and teleconferencing. In 1972 Brand coined the term "personal computer." He went on to found the WELL (Whole Earth 'Lectronic Link), a teleconference system that prompted worldwide conversations about technological liberation, in 1984. Brand's friend and colleague Kevin Kelly built upon the *Whole Earth* legacy when he founded *Wired* magazine, the ultimate hub of technology and culture, in the 1990s. To understand Brand's vision is to understand the powerful confluence of hacking, making, caring, and sharing that underlies the contemporary culture of design.

1  See Fred Turner, *From Counterculture to Cyberculture: Stewart Brand, the Whole Earth Network, and the Rise of Digital Utopianism* (Chicago: University of Chicago Press, 2006).

# WHOLE EARTH CATALOG

**STEWART BRAND | 1968**

### PURPOSE

We are as gods and might as well get used to it. So far, remotely done power and glory—as via government, big business, formal education, church—has succeeded to the point where gross obscure actual gains. In response to this dilemma and to these gains a realm of intimate, personal power is developing—power of the individual to conduct his own education, find his own inspiration, shape his own environment, and share his adventure with whoever is interested. Tools that aid this process are sought and promoted by the *Whole Earth Catalog*.

### FUNCTION

The *Whole Earth Catalog* functions as an evaluation and access device. With it, the user should know better what is worth getting and where and how to do the getting.

An item is listed in the *Catalog* if it is deemed:
1) Useful as a tool,
2) Relevant to independent education,
3) High quality or low cost,
4) Not already common knowledge,
5) Easily available by mail.

**WIM CROUWEL SHOOK THE WORLD OF TYPOGRAPHY BY DEVELOPING A FUNCTIONAL TYPEFACE FOR THE DISPLAY SCREEN.** Crouwel was an expressionist painter before he founded the interdisciplinary Dutch studio Total Design in 1963. Influenced by Swiss typography, particularly the Basel school, he earned the nickname "Gridnik" among his colleagues for his "frenetically" gridded work, particularly for the Stedelijk Museum.¹ In 1965 the Dutch designer visited an exhibition in Germany, where he saw the first machine for digitizing type. Amazed by the technology but horrified by the ugly version of Garamond that it produced, Crouwel insisted upon creating "a typeface suitable for the machine" rather than the other way around. The controversial result: New Alphabet, an experimental typeface limited to horizontal, vertical, and small diagonal strokes that he developed specifically for cathode ray tube (CRT) technology. Each character aligned both horizontally and vertically within a tight grid. Traditional typographers hated it. Typophiles still embrace its almost indecipherable forms. Like the avant-garde designers of the early twentieth century, Crouwel explored a functional machine aesthetic. The "machine," however, no longer represented the streamlined factories of the early twentieth century but rather the direct, unequivocal language of code.

1 Wim Crouwel, interview
  by *Étapes* magazine,
  February 2007, *YouTube*,
  https://www.youtube.com/
  watch?v=I5y3px4ovxE.

# TYPE DESIGN FOR THE COMPUTER AGE

**WIM CROUWEL | 1970**

Although typography has always reflected the cultural pattern of its period, today's typefaces and typographic design are a reflection of the past, not of contemporary society. We must think in terms of our electronic media and contemporary forms of expression. A suggested approach for designing today's typography—based on a cell or unit system—is discussed and illustrated.

Leonardo da Vinci may not have been an important type designer; he was, in any case, one of the first who tried to bring letter-types into the framework of a construction. Many after him have repeatedly tried, with more or less success, to analyze the highly individual signs that letters are into a number of basic forms. In da Vinci's case it was clearly the constructor who felt the need to reduce things to simple principles; moreover, his constructions were inspired by his being a sensitive artist.

This attempt—to reproduce constructionally what the human hand created with care and devotion—never had many actual consequences for the evolution of type. Clearly, man's productivity could easily meet the existing demands, and the individual who looked a bit further stayed alone; economically there was no need.

Now, however, we have reached a period—the second half of the twentieth century—in which economic necessity has created machines capable of

**WIM CROUWEL** Early sketches of New Alphabet (circa 1965) included large diagonal strokes.

reproducing characters at a speed of several thousand per second. In 1969 Leonardo da Vinci would have been able to contribute much to the development of the typesetting machine and especially to the evolution of types for it. We can assume that da Vinci, who reflected the trend of his time with extreme sensitivity, would have evolved a highly appropriate type, a type that would not be anachronistic to the spacecraft in which the first men landed on the moon.

For the moment I shall ignore the fact that computers and CRT setting systems came into existence as a result of military needs. And I only mentioned Leonardo da Vinci (who also designed horrible war machines) to indicate that typographical development has always been closely related to a period—its techniques, its economics, its art, and its culture. As there were the Phoenicians with imprinted clay tablets, the Romans with their inscriptions in marble, the men of the Middle Ages with illustrated parchment, the men of the Renaissance with soft lead type, and the Classicist with type engraved in steel; each period with the type conforming to its need and reflecting a total cultural pattern.

We do not conform to this tendency today; our type is generally anachronistic, out of touch with our particular time. Today, for example, we should soon be able to project letters into space with the help of laser beams. We have for too long seen the typographical character as a form in itself. We have for too long practiced the writing down of these beautiful characters: in school, in our handwriting; in art school, in calligraphy and letter drawing. We have been so intent upon copying something from the past that we have forgotten to think of our own time. We are so dazzled by the beauty of the characters with which we have to do every day that we cannot bring ourselves to regard them objectively. Writing by hand is fortunately a vanishing skill. In the future it will serve only for making rapid abstract notes, which will be of no value except to the writer, and undecipherable except by him. For true communicative purposes its role is finished.

The letter type for our time will, therefore, certainly not be based on the written or drawn examples of the past. The type that will now come into existence will be determined by the contemporary man who is familiar with the computer and knows how to live with it. Likewise, this type will be determined by the art of the present time, with its rapidly changing character in which aesthetic values are given a totally different interpretation. The type will be determined by the contemporary cultural pattern of which we have as yet only a partial view, but that each of us senses, and in which we participate; a period with a tremendous urge for renewal.

Our computers work according to the very simple system of yes or no, 1 or 2. The memory of a computer is an assembly of cells, charged positively or negatively. This assembly of cells, so similar to the composition of organisms and to the structure of our entire society, could be a new starting point for the development of new characters. I do not know whether this ought to be letters or pictograms; in principle I speak of communication symbols. Symbols in every form can be constructed with these cells and even spatial symbols are possible. The computer does not have a merely two-dimensional "output," but a three-dimensional possibility. The cells may be strung together in certain patterns; this pattern construction determines the form of the symbol.

In our present arsenal of forms one finds many corresponding expressions—the clearest in contemporary architecture—all based on the principle of many small units, together shaping the form. For example: the honeycomb, certain architectural studies by Konrad Wachsmann, the geodesic domes of Buckminster Fuller, and Habitat at the Montreal Expo. No matter which computer-aided system one applies, the cell principle seems to me a correct starting point, just as was the papyrus stamp, the goose quill, or the engraver's tool.

Although the cell form is important for the arrangement of patterns, I use the expression "dots" as an example for convenience's sake. If we compose a classical letterform with these dots, you will notice that there is something happening. The letter cannot be dotted, cannot be screened; that is incompatible with its appearance. In principle nothing is changed when one takes four hundred dots to the centimeter instead of twenty. Apparently everything is in order, but the screening has been done. It remains a concealed affront! It is against the classical letterform.

One can compare this to another example. In the nineteenth century when cast iron was discovered, we were proud of the fact that we could imitate everything in cast iron, indistinguishable to the naked eye from the original article. By means of this, beautiful wood carvings and sculpture were copied for architectural purposes. We soon saw that this was the wrong approach. In the same way we will doubtless stop the reproduction of Bodoni and Garamond on the supersonic machines. It is an error!

The assembly of cells that is so marvelously adapted to the computer principle will have to lead to a specific sign language. Taking into account the uniformity of the cells, an equilateral form is perhaps the most desirable for these signs—an enlarged cell form, as it were. It is also desirable in view of a variable typography. Every conceivable combination in all directions can then be achieved. I would like to adopt some sort of vocabulary agreement to facilitate understanding.

Together the cells form the signs, I would call these *nuclei*; together these nuclei form words or concepts, I would call these *units*; these units form the *communication*. A communication is an assembly of units, and a unit is an assembly of nuclei. Giving form to a communication is therefore typography. Typography, according to this system of nuclei, will be very clearly defined. The construction of this typography could be much freer, could even be developed in the third dimension; while, on the other hand, the form would appear far more systematic and harmonious than in traditional typography. It will probably lead to equilateral two- or three-dimensional sizes if we assume that the cellform determines the form of the nucleus, the nuclear forms determine the forms of the units, and the forms of the units determine the form of the communication. The increase or decrease in size of a specific type sign, a specific nucleus, means that a greater or smaller number of cells is involved.

A result of this is that a freely drawn curved line changes its shape in principle with every increase or decrease in size. Again I say "in principle" because with four hundred cells per centimeter, this could not be observed by the naked eye. The fact remains, however, that there is an unacceptable change of the sign in every size, while the meaning remains unchanged. This would mean that all straight lines of 90 degrees or 45 degrees could serve as the basis for the construction of the nuclei. These directions do not change and are the most regular in the cell construction. Straight lines with other angles—such as 60 degrees or 30 degrees—could possibly also be considered.

A letter type was designed two years ago as a basis for discussion along these lines in which a correspondence between reproductions of types and of illustrations was effected. After all, illustrations have for many years been reproduced by means of the multiplication of dots, even though in this case different dot sizes are used. An illustration could just as well be reproduced by same-sized dots, only a far greater density than has been possible so far is needed. It is a matter of the refinement of printing techniques. It would be ideal when illustrations and type could be handled in the same way. The typographer would then have innumerable possibilities at his disposal, and complete integration of illustration and text could be realized.

For the "total" typography, which then becomes possible and which might even assume spatial dimensions, simple grids would have to be constructed. These grids may be compared to the structure in architecture, in which housing units can be placed as required. A grid is the invisible network of lines into which signs and illustrations are placed as required. And since the computer is able to carry out spatial calculation, this typography could also achieve an extra dimension, which very soon would also be completely visible from all sides in space. Just as holography is already showing.

The laser beam in typography. I wonder if we could then still maintain the term typography.

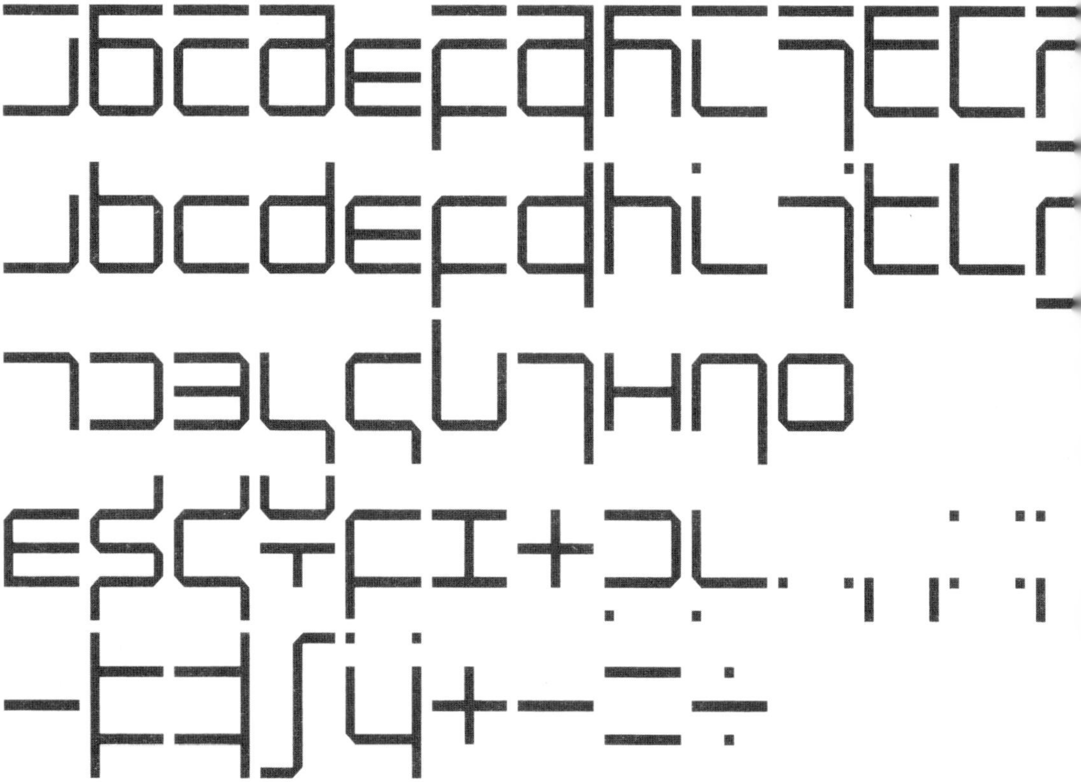

**NEW ALPHABET** An experimental alphabet designed by Wim Crouwel for the CRT technology used by early data display screens, 1967.

**SOL LEWITT PRIVILEGED CONCEPT OVER EXECUTION.** A founder of both minimal art and conceptual art, he established parameters through which serial work could emerge. In the 1950s LeWitt worked briefly in New York City as a graphic designer, first for *Seventeen* magazine and later for I. M. Pei's architectural firm. He did not relish this experience but did develop a fascination for typography. In 1968 LeWitt made the first of his well-known wall drawings. In this body of work, he developed specific guidelines or diagrams that provided instructions for another person to draw a two-dimensional work directly on walls. To put this in more technological terms, LeWitt encoded the process of a work of art, thereby divorcing the concept from the manifestation of form. Just as a programmer creates a series of steps for a computer to follow, LeWitt provided steps for a human to follow. LeWitt, however, played with the ambiguity of text, purposefully carving out space in his instructions for the human executor to make individual decisions. As a result, each rendition of a wall drawing is unique. And each rendition speaks to us about the push-pull of logic and intuition.

# DOING WALL DRAWINGS

**SOL LEWITT | 1971**

The artist conceives and plans the wall drawing. It is realized by draftsmen (the artist can act as his own draftsman); the plan (written, spoken, or drawn) is interpreted by the draftsman.

There are decisions that the draftsman makes, within the plan, as part of the plan. Each individual, being unique, if given the same instructions would understand them differently and would carry them out differently.

The artist must allow various interpretations of his plan. The draftsman perceives the artist's plan, then reorders it to his experience and understanding.

The draftsman's contributions are unforeseen by the artist, even if he, the artist, is the draftsman. Even if the same draftsman followed the same plan twice, there would be two different works of art. No one can do the same thing twice.

The artist and the draftsman become collaborators in making the art.

Each person draws a line differently and each person understands words differently.

Neither lines nor words are ideas, they are the means by which ideas are conveyed.

The wall drawing is the artist's art, as long as the plan is not violated. If it is, then the draftsman becomes the artist and the drawing would be his work of art, but art that is a parody of the original concept.

The draftsman may make errors in following the plan. All wall drawings contain errors, they are part of the work.

The plan exists as an idea but needs to be put into its optimum form. Ideas of wall drawings alone are contradictions of the idea of wall drawings.

The explicit plan should accompany the finished wall drawing. They are of equal importance.

**SOL LEWITT** Installation view of the exhibition *Sol LeWitt* at the Museum of Modern Art, New York, February 3-April 4, 1978. Photo: Katherine Keller.

**MAX BILL** *USA baut*, 1945. Bill believed in precision, order, and structure, yet he never lost sight of the human at the center of each project. In response to a questionnaire sent out by the editors of *Bauhaus* magazine in 1928, Bill wrote: "The highest demand for human beings in a social regard is: personal freedom....This is why technology is so important. Technology should liberate the people, but through the political system technology has subjugated people even more."

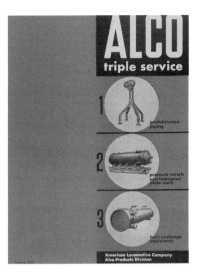

*clockwise from top left:* **LADISLAV SUTNAR** Pages from Sweet's Catalog Service, 1941–60: ALCO Triple Service; Atlantic Flexible Metal Hose; and Cuno Continuously Cleanable Filters for Product Designers. Sutnar used his work for Sweet's Catalog Service as a testing ground for the most effective organization of information in the postwar industrial age. He remarks in *Visual Design in Action:* "All of the conventional and other nonfunctional approaches prove inadequate when tested by industry's new need for a dynamic system of information design. They fail to meet the requirements for functional information flow so necessary for fast perception."

**KARL GERSTNER**
*Compendium for Literates:
A System of Writing* (MIT Press,
1974). On the book jacket,
*Compendium* is described as "a
system established on structural
criteria. And, in anticipation of
the not-so-distant future, supplies
parameters for the programming
of electronically controlled, i.e.,
computer typography." Gerstner's
fascination with typography and
computers has played out repeatedly
over his career. While working for
IBM in the 1980s, Gerstner read
about famed computer scientist
Donald Knuth's early work with
Metafont. Intrigued by the concept
of mathematically programmed
letterforms, Gerstner contacted
Knuth to collaborate on an original
typeface for IBM. Although Knuth
was willing, the project eventually fell
apart because of time constraints.

**SOL LEWITT** *Plan for a Wall Drawing*, 1969. Over the course of his career, LeWitt created more than 1,270 wall drawings. The parameters of the process, or instructions, create the concept from which each form manifests. Individuals still enact LeWitt's wall drawings today, continuing to follow his instructions, each bringing a unique subjectivity to the process.

PLAN FOR WALL DRAWING / PAULA COOPER GALLERY / MAY 15,16 1969

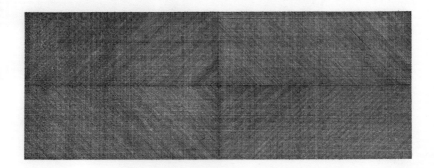

The wall drawing was executed by Adrian Piper, Terry Otter and Sol LeWitt on the south wall of the smaller room of the Paula Cooper Gallery, 96 Prince St. It is part of an exhibition for the benefit of the Art Workers Coalition and was compiled by Lucy Lippard. This drawing is 16'6" x 6', composed of four sections, each 3'9" x 3', and was drawn with 9H graphite sticks. The drawing is the width of the wall, the height of each section, 3', is dictated by the maximum length that a line can be easily drawn using a 30°-right triangle as a guide. Each of the four sections has three crossing lines superimposed on one another (vertical, horizontal, diagonal left to right, and diagonal right to left-45°), representing the basic directions that lines can be drawn. These lines are drawn as lightly and as close together as possible (1/16"). The tonality of the drawing should be equal since there are an equal number of lines in each segment. However the properties of the wall, in some cases, dictate the darkness of the lines (e.g. if there is a trace of grease or foreign substance, or if the wall bulges out). The pressure exerted by the draftsman is not always equal, nor is the distance between lines always the same accounting for darker areas. These deviations are acceptable and beyond the scope of planning, they are inherent in the method. The wall drawing is perceived first as a light toned mass light enough to preserve the integrity of the wall plane and second a collection of lines. Neither the wall drawing, the drawing in ink, or the photographic record of the wall drawing is definitive but all are of equal importance. The wall drawing is temporary and will be removed at the occasion of the Paula Cooper Gallery. Sol LeWitt May 20, 1969

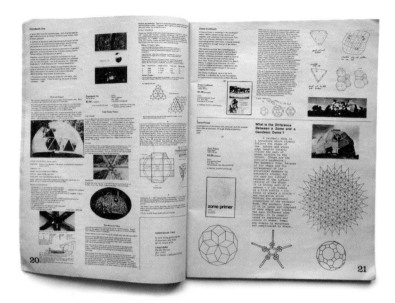

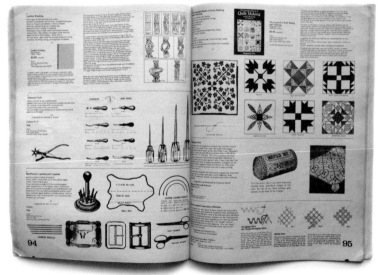

**STEWART BRAND** *Whole Earth Catalog: Access to Tools* (Portola Institute, 1970). Brand believes in the power of amateurs. In "We Are as Gods," he claims that the *Whole Earth Catalog*, created with an IBM Selectric Composer, is the earliest example of desktop publishing.[1]

1 Stewart Brand, "We Are as Gods," Winter 1998, http://www.wholeearth. com/issue/1340/article/189/we.are. as.gods (accessed July 1, 2015).

**WIM CROUWEL** Poster for the Stedelijk Museum, Amsterdam, 1968. As a modernist, Crouwel looked to materials to guide form. The structured rigor of his approach lent itself to the limitations of computing. The natural grid of the screen fit perfectly with his existing Swiss style gridded methodology.

# RESISTING CENTRAL PROCESSING

**STEVE JOBS INTRODUCED THE ORIGINAL MACINTOSH COMPUTER IN 1984. WHILE SOME DESIGNERS SAW NO USE FOR THIS NEWFANGLED TOOL, MANY OTHERS TOOK ONE LOOK AT ITS INTUITIVE GUI AND PURCHASED THEIR OWN MACHINE.** Desktop publishing and multimedia became buzzwords of the 1980s and '90s. Laser printers and video cameras put production tools into designers' hands, leading to more iterative, user-tested approaches to work. Alternatives to mass production suddenly became possible, an opportunity explored in depth by Muriel Cooper in her Visible Language Workshop at MIT. The digitization of type led to a surge in type design. Just van Rossum and Erik van Blokland of LettError began to investigate what happens when type shifts from a static form to a set of parameters. Freed from the need for expensive equipment and specialists, designers including Zuzana Licko and P. Scott Makela—much to the dismay of Swiss style modernists—looked beyond traditional forms to bitmapped shapes and flexible, layered, chaotic images. As mass-market personal computers spread across the United States, computer scientist Alan Kay, pioneer of the GUI, advocated for a society of individuals who could code. He urged the public to seize control of the computer medium, encouraging people to use computers to generate their own materials and tools. A disciplinary debate had been ignited that continues today: should designers learn to code?

**THE MACINTOSH COMPUTER**
This early desktop computer brought computation to the masses. Designers such as April Greiman, Zuzana Licko, and P. Scott Makela seized the potential of this crazy new machine.

FOR TWENTY-SIX YEARS SHARON POGGENPOHL EDITED THE PREEMINENT DESIGN JOURNAL *VISUAL LANGUAGE* (1987-2013). DURING THIS SAME PERIOD SHE COORDINATED THE PhD IN DESIGN PROGRAM AT THE CHICAGO INSTITUTE OF TECHNOLOGY, AND LATER SHE INITIATED AN INTERACTION DESIGN PROGRAM AT HONG KONG POLYTECHNIC UNIVERSITY. In 1983–a year before Steve Jobs unveiled the original Macintosh–she urged designers to ally with computers. As she explains in the essay below: "The cycle changes–conceive an idea, the computer generates form alternatives. We evaluate and select. The seams are more apparent. Time is abbreviated. The realm of possibility expands." Poggenpohl understood that technology would fundamentally alter communication. To stay relevant in this shifting landscape, designers would need to be computer literate and research knowledgeable. Using this double-edged sword, they could bridge art and science, an effective stance for the future of the discipline. Over the course of her career Poggenpohl's voice rose against the anti-intellectual clamor that often surfaces in the graphic design profession, as she succeeded in putting her words into action with her leadership of *Visual Language* and her tireless advancement of graduate design study.

# CREATIVITY AND TECHNOLOGY

### SHARON POGGENPOHL | 1983

The gap between design and the new visual computer technology is expanding. Three forces are at work that make it difficult to bridge the gap: attitudes within computer science itself, graphic designers' ambiguous role and professional goals, and lethargy within the university programs that prepare the next generation of designers.

### PROBLEM ONE: ATTITUDES WITHIN COMPUTER SCIENCE

A considerable amount of mysticism surrounds the computer and its use. Certainly its special language is no small barrier; easy entry into computer literacy is impossible. Within computer science departments at the university, the attitude is generally, "Learn my language and then we'll talk."

It's easy for computer scientists to sidestep the designer. They have technical prowess—they own the ballpark. The designers can't even play the game. The result is that powerful design tools are being put in the hands of the visual novice. What happens to visual values when the visually illiterate use the tools and designers who are illiterate in terms of the computer abdicate their responsibility?

## PROBLEM TWO: GRAPHIC DESIGNERS' AMBIGUOUS ROLE

Designers remain ambiguous about a definition of graphic design. If you can't decide where you are, how can you decide what resources you have and how to begin moving in a new direction? Graphic designers might define their activity in any of the following ways: translator of verbal ideas into visual form, technical expert who prepares art for reproduction, psychologist who sells ideas via commercial art, aesthetic expert who orders space in an appropriate way, or solver of communication problems. Most definitions share a concern with visual attractiveness and "print"; they take a narrow, parochial view of the scope of graphic design.

## PROBLEM THREE: DESIGN EDUCATION

Design programs within the university clearly recognize the need to prepare students for creative computer use. But the obstacles to accomplishing this goal are substantial. Lack of funds to acquire basic equipment is one such obstacle. Sending students over to use equipment in Computer Science is difficult, although this is the general solution. However, the student has to operate on alien turf and solicit advice and help from individuals who do not understand design, so the results are fuzzy.

Yet another obstacle is that there are few design educators who have computer experience and can translate it into new possibilities for students. A few individuals do have one foot in design and the other in computer science. They are rare, yet they are the vehicles for bridging the gap.

Educators are caught in the trap of feeding an existing profession with bottom-run entrants cut in the model of specialist rather than generalist. However, their interest and commitment is to educating "change agents" who will move the profession beyond its current understanding and limitations.

This tension between the profession and education can be productive. But, in these conservative times when risk taking is unattractive and the economy unpredictable, the balance tends to shift in favor of fulfilling the profession's perceived needs rather than toward preparing students for the future.

## MEETING THE CHALLENGE

Design can accept the challenge and close the gap between design practice and the new technology. But to do so, the designer must reorient; move from specialist to generalist; design a process rather than a special, isolated object. We have a head start because we understand visual systems and the issues surrounding visual language.

FUNDAMENTALLY, DESIGN—THE PROCESS OF BRINGING INTO EXISTENCE THE UNKNOWN OR INVISIBLE—ENVISIONS THE FUTURE.

SHARON POGGENPOHL
"Plain Talk: About Learning
and a Life...in Design"
2003

## THE NEED FOR NEW STRATEGIES

We need to do a better job educating graphic designers. Exposure to problem-solving strategies developed largely by architects and industrial designers need to complement the graphic designer's intuitive skills. As designers grapple with complex problems, they need more powerful strategies.

- Research skills become more important as we learn to design from an information base rather than blindly following the tradition of solution. An information base helps to define problems in more complete and unique ways that can assist us in examining human needs, technological possibilities, or ways to extend visual language.
- We need to analyze design problems in terms of communication theory and perceptual psychology.
- We need to become computer literate. We can select our literacy level, from user of existing programs to creative designer of new visual programs.
- Team experience becomes an important element in design education because we will not be working alone on complex projects.
- Finally, in the low-threat environment of the university, we need to encourage risk taking and tackle nontrivial design projects that help the student examine large communication issues rather than craft pedestrian objects that imitate a tradition.

Graphic design is entering a transitional period, and transitions are both difficult and provocative. In fact, the environment within which communication design now exists is already changing. Information, once laboriously codified in book form, now exists in a fluid computer context. (It is as though a net or dimensional grid of densely interrelated ideas replace the linear string of the book.) Our ability to pull appropriate information together, to synthesize it, enhances the information base for our communication problems. Information is less precious than before, and it is more accessible if we are computer literate.

The computer alters the designer's form environment. If there is a mystique associated with design, it is that we make "form"; we create a visual entity from scratch. We imagine it and we physically make it happen. Form making requires a visual sensitivity nurtured over time. It is the integration of intellect and hand skills; we think as we make. The cycle of action, feedback, evaluation, and adjustment is seamless. The time for one visual entity to take form can be considerable. We learn to edit ideas before they take form; we eliminate certain avenues as too laborious and complex for development. The computer dramatically alters this set of expectations. It can quickly play out hundreds of alternatives—show radically divergent form ideas, or subtle form change.

## THE COMPUTER AS ALLY

The cycle changes—conceive an idea, the computer generates form alternatives. We evaluate and select. The seams are more apparent. Time is abbreviated. The realm of possibility expands. Imagine we have any typeface at our disposal on an interactive computer system. We can use simple directions to effect change by means of asking for certain operations to be performed on the type; we can fragment, distort, incline, change weight, etc. Consider all the permutations of a logotype we can easily run through. We are limited only by our imagination. We conceive of a visual game—the computer helps us play it out in great detail. Will we find new, more elegant form? It is too soon to tell.

The qualities of good design can be systematically extended. Design increasingly is considered in relation to systems of things—books, signage, symbols, etc. Again, the computer is our ally. To the extent that we can define the visual program we are free to move on to other projects; we do not need to laboriously implement a system. This freedom will tax our sense of creative accomplishment. The proportion of creative time to execution time changes.

## THE CHOICE IS OURS

We can ignore these changes in the design environment, but we do so at considerable risk. Change is underway and is moving swiftly, with or without us. The choice is ours. The computer does not rob us of creative initiative; it sets us free.

RESEARCH IS BASED ON EVIDENCE THAT CAN BE ANALYZED AND SYNTHESIZED TO GET AN ANSWER TO THE QUESTION BEING ASKED.

**SHARON POGGENPOHL**
"Design Research, Building a Culture from Scratch"
2010

**IN 1986 APRIL GREIMAN POWERFULLY DEMONSTRATED TO A DOUBTFUL EAST COAST GRAPHIC DESIGN ESTABLISHMENT THAT COMPUTERS WERE INDEED VALUABLE TOOLS.** When asked to author an issue of *Design Quarterly*, she used the provided honorarium to buy MacVision, a combination of software and hardware that allowed her to import still images from a video camera. Using MacVision and a dot-matrix printer, Greiman painstakingly composited the issue.[1] Rather than a traditional retrospective, the resulting magazine folded out into a life-size poster of Greiman's nude body layered with imagery and text. The dense poster traces a personal history of technology while questioning the boundaries between art and design.

Never quelled by computation, Greiman bought her first Macintosh in 1984 after hearing a lecture by Alan Kay at the inaugural TED conference.[2] The influence of her technological daring cannot be ignored, but she is more than a technophile. A student of Wolfgang Weingart, Greiman is a key figure in the introduction of New Wave style to the United States. Her expressive hybrid designs splice digital with physical to probe universals of the human condition. Before networked culture permeated our lives, Greiman used budding technology to connect us through color, symbology, and mythology.

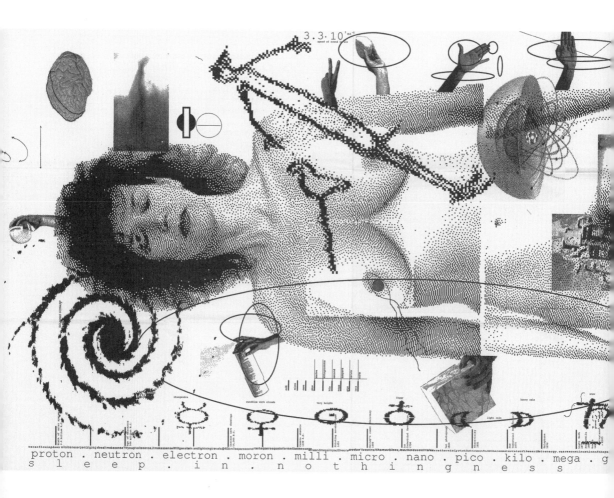

1 April Greiman, "Think About
What You Think About"
(lecture, San Jose State
University, February 7, 2012),
https://www.youtube.com/
watch?v=Ek5mu1wY8c0.

2 April Greiman, interview by
Josh Smith, *idsgn*, September 11,
2009, http://idsgn.org/posts/
design-discussions-april-greiman-
on-trans-media/.

# DOES IT MAKE SENSE?

## APRIL GREIMAN | 1986

So I'm walking through the English Garden with Andreas—and I mention
the idea (duality) of order and chaos. So, he tips me off to the latest philosoph-
ical twist—chaos is simply a man/mind-made invention that frankly doesn't
exist! I think about this and I say…yea, come to think about it, in seeing a
computer model of fractal geometry, things that appear without structures,
such as clouds and mountains, are in fact orderly processes. While on the
surface, things seem irregular and chaotic, when you break down the parts, in
reality they are more and more modular and ordered. The more finitely we
perceive them, the more their inherent order becomes apparent.

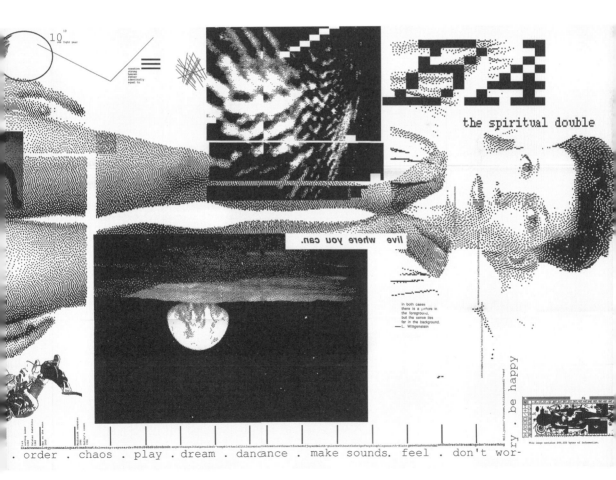

**DURING HER TWENTY-YEAR LEADERSHIP OF THE VISIBLE LANGUAGE WORKSHOP (VLW), WHICH BECAME PART OF THE MIT MEDIA LAB IN 1985, MURIEL COOPER AND HER STUDENTS TORE DOWN WALLS—LITERALLY—BETWEEN DESIGN AND PRODUCTION.** This path was set soon after the workshop began, in protest of an awkward room arrangement. Cooper's students clandestinely met in the night to break down the wall separating their workspace and the photographic prepress room next door. The resulting setup included offset printers, photocopiers, and later computers, encouraging students to tinker with the production equipment throughout the design process.[1] What happens, Cooper asks in the essay below, when the limitations imposed by mass production begin to lift? What happens when technology puts the tools of production directly into the hands of the designer? Cooper turned toward iterative and intuitive approaches to design, approaches she considered akin to those used by the sciences. As the printed page gave way to the computer screen, her research focused on interface design. At the TED conference in 1994 Cooper presented a new kind of interface—"an information landscape"—to great acclaim. Her interface allowed the user to construct meaning by flying through a screen-based nonlinear information environment. Media Lab director Nicholas Negroponte declared: "She has broken the flatland of overlapping opaque rectangles with the idea of a galactic universe."[2] Three months after her groundbreaking presentation, Cooper died unexpectedly at age sixty-eight.

1 For a wonderful discussion of Cooper's years at MIT, see David Reinfurt, "This Stands as a Sketch for the Future," *Dexter Sinister*, October 23, 2007, http://www.dextersinister.org/library.html?id=122.

2 Nicholas Negroponte, "Design Statement on Behalf of Muriel Cooper" (presentation, Chrysler Design Awards, 1994).

# COMPUTERS AND DESIGN

**MURIEL COOPER | 1989**

### THE NEW GRAPHIC LANGUAGES

Today's personal computer is a functional tool that mimics old tools. But the next generation of graphic computers will permit the merging of previously separate professional tools; at the same time, powerful networking, increased bandwidth, and processing capabilities will make the transition from print to electronic communication the basis of a vast industry. The primary interaction of electronic communication environments will be visual. Traditional graphic design skills will continue to be important for display and presentation, but a new interdisciplinary profession, whose practitioners will be adept in the integration of static and dynamic words and images, will be required to organize and filter information growing at an exponential rate.

In each period of our history, design and communication have evolved synchronously with the technology of the time. Each new medium has extended our sense of reality, and each has looked to its predecessor for language and conventions, referencing and adapting its characteristics until

MURIEL COOPER
Interview with
Ellen Lupton
1994

its unique capabilities can be explored and codified. Print, in its infancy, emulated the conventions of calligraphic writing on vellum; typography was modeled on the penmanship of scriptorium; images and color embellishment continued to be added to the printed page by hand, emulating the methods of the monastery.

Since the Industrial Revolution, the expanding tools of the print and broadcast technologies have made the broad dissemination of information possible. A rich and overlapping array of related design and communication fields evolved and matured rapidly in response to mass communication needs. These included graphic and typographic design, illustration, photography, multi-image design, exhibition and interior design, industrial, and environmental design. While the conventions and performance of each often overlapped, they also depended in unique ways upon the physical constraints and characteristics of their trades: reproduction tools of typography, photography, and print; slide, film, and video projection, and synchronization tools; sound making, reproduction and mixing tools, for example. As the tools of these media were honed and adapted for broader penetration and use through continuing loops of research and market testing, so were the conventions and languages, the methods of production, and the patterns of communication within each of the design fields.

Natural visual and aural languages were gradually translated into message making conventions that coupled intuitive understanding of human perception with the organization of images and words into two dimensions. Reality was filtered and organized through the limitations of the media, modifying the way we think. The restrictions of the page, the frame, the aspect ratio of the television set, the physical space of an exhibition hall, and the manufacturing tools also defined the degree to which audience or user could interact with the medium. Communication with large audiences could only be accomplished through expensive, complex media channels, traditionally controlled by the few, motivated and driven primarily by sales and advertising in the United States and often by political expediency in other parts of the world. At this scale, the filtering and editing of information became a consequence of economic control. As H. J. Liebling once quipped, "freedom of the press is guaranteed—to anyone who owns one."

In that context design is interactive and recurrent. It is also focused and goal dependent. The beginning and end of the process are clearly defined and demand conceptual clarity and closure. This limits evolutionary interaction with the medium and the audience or user and requires generalized solutions for large audiences. It is counter to a more intuitive or evolutionary approach to the thinking and problem solving associated with the arts and research, which depends on constant testing and refinement, and encourages lyric leaps.

At the frontiers of expression, unencumbered by the restraints of the marketplace, artists and designers have pushed the time and space limitations of print and mass production with experimental works in limited editions. The traditions of binding, of the page, of sequence, of materials of the package, of audience participation, have all been violated in an effort to break away from the tyranny of a fixed set of relationships....

Artists and designers have often become their own authors and producers, gathering to themselves the autonomy that allows control over all aspects of an idea, breaking away from the limitations of mass production. Self-publishing centers created by artists or art schools are equipped with traditional reproduction tools normally found in commercial printing establishments and generate creative publishing alternatives for limited editions. Xerography and computer typesetting and walk-in copy centers with increasingly sophisticated typesetting, printing, and binding facilities allow a form of on-demand printing and inexpensive self-publishing in limited editions. Desktop publishing coupled with high-resolution typesetting challenges the mass-production paradigm even further.

### THE GRAPHICS COMPUTER AS TOOL AND AS MEDIUM

The history of the computer as a new medium follows the pattern of new media emulating old. Very early, its capacity to transform information from analog to digital and back, shape it at processing speeds that resemble the way we think, and maintain massive amounts of data in memory provided us with fast and effective tools that emulate many of the old ones in every professional medium. Early digital paint systems were modeled on physical, analog brushes; the language and behavior of physical oil and watercolor painting were laid on top of a digital world like a varnish.

Computer graphics, image processing, computer vision, and robotics required huge computing power and were used only in high-cost research environments. Mathematics provided the tools to model physical processes, to visualize complex scientific data, to animate space travel, and to simulate real-time flight. Large and very expensive mainframe computers dominated the industry well into the 1970s and continue to play a key role in many corporate and institutional systems.

I HAD A MISSION: DESIGN WAS A WAY OF LIFE. THAT WAS INFLUENCED BY [WALTER] GROPIUS, [GYÖRGY] KEPES, HERBERT READ, EVEN [JOHN] DEWEY, WHO WAS STILL AROUND THEN. PLUS [MARCEL] DUCHAMP WAS VERY IMPORTANT, THE FRENCH, GERTRUDE STEIN.

MURIEL COOPER
Interview with
Ellen Lupton
1994

The advantages of the computer for expensive, high-resolution graphic arts soon became clear. Computer typography and layout developed in parallel with the visual computer. Word and image were merged later, when high-end designer stations were developed as a logical extension of the prepress production process. The creative potential of these machines soon attracted designers and artists. Predictably, the work was traditional but took advantage of the machine's capability for fast and seemingly infinite transformations that would have been impossible with traditional physical tools. New digital techniques, such as "cloning" and changing color matrices, were quickly exploited. Use of the machines was not easy. It required the help of operators or, in the case of research environments, the help of programmers. And use was expensive on an hourly basis. A few hardy, committed visionaries began to learn programming. A significant number of programmers began to experiment with personal graphic ideas. It was only a matter of time until these tools migrated into the creative domain. The cost effectiveness of connecting such prepress tools to the creative part of the graphic arts and communication industry was soon apparent.

**MURIEL COOPER**
Meeting with a group at MIT in her notoriously bare feet, 1970s.

At this stage the term "user-friendly" was unheard of. A few dedicated designers understood the potential of the future of the graphic computer and began to design interface graphics. Most of the work was static and used traditional print-design principles. Much of this work was done in office "automation," where productivity and efficiency were critical. The work was difficult since most of the machines did not yet have sufficient resolution or speed to provide anything but a crude approximation of print quality. Typography continued to be separate from image in graphic arts systems, following the production model of offset technology; and images were only merged with text at the end of the production cycle in newspaper layout and editing systems.

Input and output were available, but costly. Some experimental prototypes were capable of capturing real-time images from the outside world and of producing prints of the completed images. These, coupled with the programmatic capabilities of the computer, an integrated set of image-processing tools, and anti-aliased typography, promised a complete graphics environment for the creative artist and designer.

Personal computers were introduced into the business and education markets in the late 1970s. The goals of computer-aided education and the automated, paperless office helped to lay the groundwork. Word processing and spreadsheets became paradigms for direct manipulation, ease of use, and a productive way of accomplishing traditional tasks. Video games dramatized the potential for interactive graphics. Technological growth and the industry's drive to saturate the professional and consumer markets drove down the price of memory to the point that color, graphics, and typography, with greatly improved resolution and input and output devices, became affordable and usable. "Input-output devices," tools such as printers and scanners, allow images, text, or sound to be digitized into the computer from the outside world (input); and the computer provides "hard copy" in the form of print, slides, or videotape (output).

Desktop publishing emerged, almost unintentionally, from the union of the laser writer and good typography. The Macintosh, the first viable graphic design tool, rapidly became the computer of choice for graphic design, primarily because it supports professional work with enhanced speed and reduced cost of typography in a reasonable work environment. While it mimics the patterns and purpose of existing design tools, it changes the patterns of production dependency. Desktop publishing is a transitional phenomenon that has transformed the graphic arts industry by putting production tools into the hands of professionals as well as nonprofessionals. An industry of desktop publishing has blossomed overnight and given birth to magazines, books, and workshops for new cottage-industry publishing entrepreneurs and new computer users. Computer and business magazines have articles on design, and design magazines inform their readers about computers. These are early symptoms of massive changes in professional and production patterns that will result in new interdisciplinary approaches to communication....

It is not yet clear that the computer is changing the way people think about design, except to the extent that it saves time and money and provides some experimental tools whose cost would otherwise be prohibitive. At the very least, in this phase the computer may allow more time for creativity, experimentation, and some preliminary crossover into three-dimensional imaging and animation by the more adventurous.

A number of designers have become consultants for businesses and schools to help in the building of appropriate systems and to set up training programs. A few designers have been working with the computer itself as a design problem. A small but growing group has coupled design and programming knowledge to influence big players in the development of new design roles, futures, and methods.

## INTEGRATION AND INTERACTION

Mixing media on any scale is complex and may result in changing or modifying media characteristics. Some mass media incorporate characteristics of others. Animation, film, and television are examples of communication media that are both static and dynamic. A television commercial often combines written and spoken words in a disjointed or simultaneous presentation of the same information. Such redundancy helps to emphasize points in different time frames as well as support handicapped viewers. A spoken name lasts only as long as it takes to speak it and is only as expressive as the voice of the speaker. Jingles and tunes have been developed to extend sound into memorable aural trademarks. A name that is graphic and visual endures and can be embedded with complex symbolic and metaphorical associations and expressions not possible with aural messages. Aural and visual messages when mixed together can result in far more powerful messages, as recently witnessed in rock videos or campaign commercials.

But visual communications in the publishing and entertainment worlds, large or small, traditional or experimental, are closed and passive. The writing and designing of printed works depend on beginnings and endings and clear-cut linear and nonvariable structures. There is no publishing without closure. The reader's participation is limited to choosing when and where one may read or view, delve in or out, scan or flip.

Designing and producing film and animation since the advent of sound is by nature multimedia. While it is dynamic, its interactive capabilities are limited. Videotape provides the viewer with some of the "flipping" control that a book or magazine provides, insofar as one may fast-forward and review. Audiotape and videotape recorders allow the relatively easy excerpting and editing that a Xerox machine provides and in limited ways lets the audience reshape the works to individual needs. A world of authorship is open to the owner of a video camera and tape recorder.

Home video games provide a controlled interaction that tempts the viewer to want more control in all television watching. The cordless remote control gives rise to quick channel hopping and a sense of simultaneity. The viewer is able to watch up to a dozen programs simultaneously without losing a single story line or commercial. Umpteen cable channels suggest that audience and community control might provide better programming. The phenomenon of the video rental and purchase business allows the viewer programming control without advertising. For the fabled yuppie the Saturday-night grocery bag is incomplete without weekend videotapes. The computer that was bought

I WAS CONVINCED THAT THE LINE BETWEEN REPRODUCTION TOOLS AND DESIGN WOULD BLUR WHEN INFORMATION BECAME ELECTRONIC AND THAT THE LINES BETWEEN DESIGNER AND ARTIST, AUTHOR AND DESIGNER, PROFESSIONAL AND AMATEUR, WOULD ALSO DISSOLVE.

MURIEL COOPER
Muriel Cooper Memorial
Exhibition Pamphlet
1994

for the kids' schooling, or for word processing, is equipped with a modem and one can tap into primitive but interactive and lively bulletin boards, videotext shopping, and the stock exchange.

## DESIGN INTEGRATION PRECEDENTS AND PIONEERS

Multi-image or audio-visual design is very close to theater and performance, and in fact often incorporates it, integrating media such as film and slides, sound and music. Like performance, this requires complex management of different technologies based on synchronized scoring or scripting within a predetermined, common time frame. Like performance, it depends heavily on three-dimensional space and does not translate well into film or videotape.

Examples of cross-media thinking abound in the history of design and have precedent in other art forms. Live opera is an example of a real-time multimedia event for large audiences. In the apocryphal and popular film *Amadeus*, Mozart tries to describe a revolutionary passage in *Don Giovanni* where twenty voices simultaneously express individual yet coherent melodies and messages that together convey the meaning of the scene and the relationships of the parts. The Bauhaus, the futurists, the Russian avant-garde, the Dadaists, the surrealists, and the performance artists of 1950s Happenings all explored the synthesis of communication media for a more interactive experience.

László Moholy-Nagy wrote that the illiterate of the future would be the person who couldn't take a photograph. His vision was holistic. His photography and movies explored the abstract and formal issues of the static and dynamic aspects of photography and the cinema, and their relationship to text. His diagrammatic notational score for the *Dynamic of the Metropolis* explores visual and verbal means of interrelating the different time frames of sound and moving image in the print medium. In fact, the score itself becomes a piece of meta-art. It is not hard to imagine Moholy using a computer. György Kepes, in *Language of Vision* and other writings, is eloquent on the interconnectedness of art, technology, and design, and the need to refresh language to reflect the changing realities of life....

Karl Gerstner, who successfully straddles the world of art and design and was an original member of Das Freundes+, wrote the classic, unfortunately out of print, *Designing Programmes* (1964), which explores the structure of design as programmed systems and resultant processes rather than as unique product. This book has a Xeroxed underground life of its own and is just beginning to be seen not only as an homage to the grid but as a way of thinking that permeates all forms of human and natural design, one that is particularly appropriate to future computer design and art.

The literature of art and technology is full of experimental works that explore the relationship of human experience to technology, in which the machine is the subject, the collaborator, or antihero. Such seminal works as Oskar Schlemmer's *Ballets Triadisches* (1922) and Ludwig Hirschfeld-Mack's pioneering works in the interdependent generation of light and sound in his *Reflected-Light Compositions* produced at the Weimar Bauhaus (1922) have been followed by a number of innovations in art and technology by such artists as John Cage, Otto Piene, Philip Glass, and Robert Wilson.[3] New creative generations continue to expand the tools with which to engage idea, audience, and machine. The personal computer and related electronic devices have become powerful new tools with which to explore these complex relationships expressively.

3  The original version of this essay incorrectly referenced "Oskar Schlemmer's *Ballet Mecanique* (1923)."

While the next phase of computer workstations will be dedicated to individual design professions, be they graphic, architectural, or engineering, the integration of the tools of those and all other professions is an inevitable consequence, which promises great challenges and changes for the design professions. The merging of media in an electronic communication environment and the emergence of multimedia workstations in the workplace and the home will result from improved, integrated technologies. Increased technological capabilities will enable the smooth flow of multimedia information throughout the electronic community....

The idea of visualizing and modeling the physical environment as a metaphor in the computer is transitional. It appears to work effectively as a comforting introduction to a seemingly flat and mysterious world. The use of icons such as file folders and trash barrels that stand for programs and move you into other parts of a program help to establish a model of the real world. But in fact, it is not the real world, and at some point on the learning curve moving iconic metaphors around is as tedious as rummaging through filing cabinets. At that point the user understands that the computer is a medium different from the physical world, one that offers the power of abstraction. As computers become more powerful and teleconferencing allows sending real-time video of people, complex issues of workplace communication will arise. The old notion of workplace and home being one and the same is returning. Before the industrial revolution people worked in or near home and there was less schism between work and family living. Computers and networking make it possible to work almost as well at home as at work. Yet the dimension of interaction with others, critical to most work, must be resolved to make that form viable today.

**WHEN ZUZANA LICKO FIRST SAT DOWN IN FRONT OF A MACINTOSH COMPUTER IN 1984, SHE EMBRACED IT AS HER OWN.** Using a single small machine sitting on her desk, she seized upon the potential to merge design and production into one complete process. Together with her partner, Rudy VanderLans, she launched Emigre Fonts and *Emigre* magazine; Licko focused on type design, and VanderLans ran the editorial. They called themselves the "New Primitives." Licko began designing type directly on the computer at a time when the design establishment saw little use for a machine that produced coarse, limited aesthetic forms. Introduced to computers at a young age by her father, a biomathematician, Licko had taken an entry-level programming class while at Berkeley; there she also studied with interface designer Aaron Marcus. She enjoyed the low-res restrictions of the computer screen and early printers, viewing the resulting bitmapped aesthetic as truly breaking ground rather than anachronistically trying to re-create classic forms in a new medium. Her first three bitmapped typefaces, Emperor, Emigre, and Oakland, shocked the design world. Heavily critiqued as illegible, ugly, and poorly crafted, these typefaces nevertheless found a commercial success that testified to the power of their aesthetic. Licko was standing at the vanguard of the type-design frenzy that followed, an era in which digital technology shoved aside longstanding barriers of expertise and expense.

# AMBITION/FEAR

### ZUZANA LICKO AND RUDY VANDERLANS | 1989

Visions of bold-italic-outline-shadow Helvetica "Mac" tricks have sent many graphic designers running back to their T-squares and rubber cement. Knowing how and when to use computers is difficult, since we have only begun to witness their capabilities. Some designers have found computers a creative salvation from the boredom of familiar methodologies, while others have utilized this new technology to expedite traditional production processes. For this eleventh issue of Emigre we interviewed fifteen graphic designers from around the world and talked about how they work their way through the sometimes-frustrating task of integrating this new technology into their daily practices.

Computer technology provides opportunities for more specialization as well as integration. Today, less peripheral knowledge and skills are required to master a particular niche. For instance, a type designer is no longer required to be a creative mind as well as a skilled punch cutter. There is also the possibility of better communication, allowing for increased crossover between disciplines. Designers can control all aspects of production and design, no longer requiring an outside typesetter or color separator.

Text, image, and layout all exist as manifestations of the same medium, and the capability of simultaneously editing text and composing the layout will influence both design and writing styles. It is now possible for one individual to take on all functions required in publishing, including writer, editor, designer, and illustrator, thus bringing together a variety of disciplines and consequently streamlining production.

The integration of previously isolated disciplines makes computer-aided design a seamless continuum of activity similar to that experienced by children. In fact, computer technology has advanced the state of graphic art by such a quantum leap into the future that it has brought the designer back to the most primitive of graphic ideas and methods. It's no wonder that our first computer-generated art usually resembles that of naive cave paintings! This return to our primeval ideas allows us to reconsider the basic assumptions made in the creative design process, bringing excitement and creativity to aspects of design that have been forgotten since the days of letterpress. We are once again faced with evaluating the basic rules of design that we formerly took for granted.

With computers many options of type combinations, sizes, and spacings can be quickly and economically reviewed. However, the time saved in the production stage is often spent viewing more design solutions. Thus today's designers must learn to discriminate intelligently among all of the choices, a task requiring a solid understanding of fundamentals.

Computer use also brings about a new breed of designers who possess the ability to integrate various media. Those individuals previously hinged between disciplines will find that digital technology allows them that crossover necessary for their personal expression. One such new area is that of digital type design. Custom typefaces can now be produced letter by letter as called for in day-by-day applications. This increases the potential for more personalized typefaces as it becomes economically feasible to create letterforms for specific uses.

By making publishing and dissemination of information faster and less expensive, computer technology has made it feasible to reach a smaller audience more effectively. It is no longer necessary to market for the lowest common denominator. There is already a growth in the birthrate of small circulation magazines and journals. Although this increases diversity and subsequently the chances of tailoring the product to the consumer, we can only hope that such abundance will not obliterate our choices by overwhelming us with options. Computers are phenomenally adept at storing information, but the current rate of its amassment is making a frightening task out of distilling knowledge from these huge data banks. Raw information becomes meaningful only when we can access it in a comprehensive manner.

The storage and transmission of text and images is also becoming progressively less physical as data is sent over phone lines and accessed through computer terminals. Digital data is easily modifiable, and it is difficult to draw the lines of ownership and copyrights. Problems of piracy are already evident in areas of program development, type design, and illustration. For example, some illustrators using digital media now opt to submit hard-copy artwork to clients rather than disk versions, fearing that their illustrations could be copied and manipulated into a misrepresentation of their work without deserved royalties. This brings up numerous previously unaddressed questions over ownership of data and our rights to use or even alter it.

But what separates digital art from its analog counterparts aesthetically? Mostly it is our perception. There is nothing intrinsically "computer-like" about digitally generated images. Low-end devices such as the Macintosh do not yield a stronger inherent style than do the high-end Scitex systems, which are often perceived as functioning invisibly and seamlessly. This merely shows what computer virgins we are. High-end computers have been painstakingly programmed to mimic traditional techniques such as airbrushing or calligraphy, whereas the low-end machines force us to deal with more original, sometimes alien, manifestations. Coarse bitmaps are no more visibly obtrusive than the texture of oil paint on a canvas, but our unfamiliarity with bitmaps causes us to confuse the medium with the message. Creating a graphic language with today's tools will mean forgetting the styles of archaic technologies and remembering the very basics of design principles.

This is perhaps the most exciting of times for designers. Digital technology is a great big unknown, and after all, a mystery is the most stimulating force in unleashing the imagination.

THE MACINTOSH COMPUTER WAS RELEASED THE YEAR I GRADUATED, AND WE (RUDY AND I) ORDERED ONE WITH OUR STUDENT DISCOUNT. I STILL REMEMBER PICKING IT UP ON CAMPUS, IN A LARGE BALLROOM, WHICH WAS STACKED TO THE RAFTERS WITH THESE MACHINES.

ZUZANA LICKO
Interview in *Étapes*
2010

**COMPUTER SCIENTIST ALAN KAY UNDERSTOOD THE COMPUTER AS A RADICALLY NEW MEDIUM THAT COULD FUNDAMENTALLY CHANGE OUR PATTERNS OF THINKING.** Influenced by Marshall McLuhan, he insisted back in the 1960s that to seize upon this power, users—all users, not only computer scientists—must be computer literate. They must be able to not only read but actually write in the medium in order to use computers to create materials and tools for others. At a 1968 graduate student conference in Illinois, with this goal in mind, Kay sketched the Dynabook, a small mobile computer with a language so simple that a child could program it. His fellow students found this idea absurd.[1] Kay, however, continued to work on making computation accessible to nonspecialists. In the early 1970s, as one of the founders of the influential Xerox Palo Alto Research Center (PARC), he pioneered a GUI that utilized overlapping windows, icons, and menus.[2] In 1979 this new symbolic interface system, along with Kay's conceptual models of the Dynabook, enamored a young Steve Jobs and inspired a bevy of mass-marketed Apple products: the Lisa, the Macintosh, and, much later, the iPad. Such products fit Kay's vision of personal computing but not his ultimate belief in empowering the public to program. Graphic designers still struggle with this possibility. Is it enough for us to use the computer as simply a tool for making? Or should we engage more deeply with the process of computation? Kay's famous statement, "The best way to predict the future is to invent it," could be a clarion call to designers everywhere to seize the power of computer literacy and, in doing so, affect the medium that increasingly dictates our livelihoods.

1 M. Mitchell Waldrop, *The Dream Machine: J. C. R. Licklider and the Revolution That Made Computing Personal* (New York: Viking, 2001), 282–83.

2 Other pioneers included Larry Tesler, Dan Ingalls, David Smith, and a number of other researchers.

# USER INTERFACE: A PERSONAL VIEW

**ALAN KAY | 1989**

Therefore, let me argue that the actual dawn of user interface design first happened when computer designers finally noticed, not just that end users had functioning minds, but that a better understanding of how those minds worked would completely shift the paradigm of interaction.

This enormous change in point of view happened to many computerists in the late sixties, especially in the ARPA research community. Everyone had their own catalyst. For me it was the FLEX machine, an early desktop personal computer of the late sixties designed by Ed Cheadle and myself.

Based on much previous work by others, it had a tablet as a pointing device, a high-resolution display for text and animated graphics, and multiple windows, and it directly executed a high-level, object-oriented, end-user simulation language. And of course it had a "user interface," but one that repelled end users instead of drawing them closer to the hearth. I recently revisited the FLEX machine design and was surprised to find how modern its components were—even a use of iconlike structures to access previous work.

But the combination of ingredients didn't gel. It was like trying to bake a pie from random ingredients in a kitchen: baloney instead of apples, ground-up Cheerios instead of flour, etc.

Then, starting in the summer of 1968, I got hit on the head randomly but repeatedly by some really nifty work. The first was just a little piece of glass at the University of Illinois. But the glass had tiny glowing dots that showed text characters. It was the first flat-screen display. I and several other grad students wondered when the surface could become large and inexpensive enough to be a useful display. We also wondered when the FLEX machine silicon could become small enough to fit on the back of the display. The answer to both seemed to be the late seventies or early eighties. Then we could all have an inexpensive powerful notebook computer—I called it a "personal computer" then, but I was thinking intimacy.

I read [Marshall] McLuhan's *Understanding Media* (1964) and understood that the most important thing about any communications medium is that message receipt is really message recovery; anyone who wishes to receive a message embedded in a medium must first have internalized the medium so it can be "subtracted" out to leave the message behind. When he said, "The medium is the message" he meant that you have to become the medium if you use it.

That's pretty scary. It means that even though humans are the animals that shape tools, it is in the nature of tools and man that learning to use tools reshapes us. So the "message" of the printed book is, first, its availability to individuals, hence, its potential detachment from extant social processes; second, the uniformity, even coldness, of noniconic type, which detaches readers from the vividness of the now and the slavery of commonsense thought to propel them into a far more abstract realm in which ideas that don't have easy visualizations can be treated.

McLuhan's claim that the printing press was the dominant force that transformed the hermeneutic Middle Ages into our scientific society should not be taken too lightly—especially because the main point is that the press didn't do it just by making books more available; it did it by changing the thought patterns of those who learned to read.

Though much of what McLuhan wrote was obscure and arguable, the sum total to me was a shock that reverberates even now. The computer is a medium! I had always thought of it as a tool, perhaps a vehicle—a much weaker

MCLUHAN'S LINE—ONE OF MY FAVORITES—IS, "WE'RE DRIVING FASTER AND FASTER INTO THE FUTURE, TRYING TO STEER BY USING ONLY THE REARVIEW MIRROR."

ALAN KAY
"Predicting
the Future"
1989

conception. What McLuhan was saying is that if the personal computer is a truly new medium, then the very use of it would actually change the thought patterns of an entire civilization. He had certainly been right about the effects of the electronic stained-glass window that was television—a remedievalizing tribal influence at best. The intensely interactive and involving nature of the personal computer seemed an antiparticle that could annihilate the passive boredom invoked by television. But it also promised to surpass the book to bring about a new kind of renaissance by going beyond static representations to dynamic simulation. What kind of a thinker would you become if you grew up with an active simulator connected, not just to one point of view, but to all the points of view of the ages represented so they could be dynamically tried out and compared? I named the notebook-sized computer idea the Dynabook to capture McLuhan's metaphor in the silicon to come.

Shortly after reading McLuhan, I visited Wally Feurzeig, Seymour Papert, and Cynthia Solomon at one of the earliest Logo tests within a school. I was amazed to see children writing programs (often recursive) that generated poetry, created arithmetic environments, and translated English into Pig Latin.[3] And they were just starting to work with the new wastepaper basket–size turtle that roamed over sheets of butcher paper, making drawings with its pen.

I was possessed by the analogy between print literacy and Logo. While designing the FLEX machine, I had believed that end users needed to be able to program before the computer could become truly theirs—but here was a real demonstration and with children! The ability to "read" a medium means you can access materials and tools created by others. The ability to "write" in a medium means you can generate materials and tools for others. You must have both to be literate. In print writing, the tools you generate are rhetorical; they demonstrate and convince. In computer writing, the tools you generate are processes; they simulate and decide.

If the computer is only a vehicle, perhaps you can wait until high school to give driver's ed on it—but if it's a medium, then it must be extended all the way into the world of the child. How to do it? Of course it has to be done on the intimate notebook-size Dynabook! But how would anyone "read" the Dynabook, let alone "write" on it?

Logo showed that a special language designed with the end user's characteristics in mind could be more successful than a random hack. How had Papert learned about the nature of children's thought? From Jean Piaget, the doyen of European cognitive psychologists. One of his most important contributions is the idea that children go through several distinctive intellectual

3  Wally Feurzeig, Seymour Papert, Cynthia Solomon, and Daniel G. Bobrow created Logo, an educational programming language, in 1967.

stages as they develop from birth to maturity. Much can be accomplished if the nature of the stages is heeded, and much grief to the child can be caused if the stages are ignored. Piaget noticed a kinesthetic stage, a visual stage, and a symbolic stage. An example is that children in the visual stage, when shown a squat glass of water poured into a tall thin one, will say there is more water in the tall thin one even though the pouring was done in front of their eyes....

The work of Papert convinced me that whatever user interface design might be, it was solidly intertwined with learning. [Jerome] Bruner convinced me that learning takes place best environmentally and roughly in stage order—it is best to learn something kinesthetically, then iconically, and finally the intuitive knowledge will be in place that will allow the more powerful but less vivid symbolic processes to work at their strongest. This led me over the years to the pioneers of environmental learning: Montessori Method, Suzuki Violin, and Tim Gallwey's *The Inner Game of Tennis*, to name just a few.

My point here is that as soon as I was ready to look deeply at the human element, and especially after being convinced that the heart of the matter lay with Bruner's multiple-mentality model, I found the knowledge landscape positively festooned with already accomplished useful work. It was like the man in Molière's *Bourgeois gentilhomme* who discovered that all his life he had been speaking prose! I suddenly remembered McLuhan: "I don't know who discovered water, but it wasn't a fish." Because it is in part the duty of consciousness to represent ourselves to ourselves as simply as possible, we should sorely distrust our commonsense self-view. It is likely that this mirrors-within-mirrors problem in which we run into a misleading commonsense notion about ourselves at every turn is what forced psychology to be one of the most recent sciences—if indeed it yet is.

Now, if we agree with the evidence that the human cognitive facilities are made up of a *doing* mentality, an *image* mentality, and a *symbolic* mentality, then any user interface we construct should at least cater to the mechanisms that seem to be there. But how? One approach is to realize that no single mentality offers a complete answer to the entire range of thinking and problem solving. User interface design should integrate them at least as well as Bruner did in his spiral curriculum ideas....

Finally, in the sixties a number of studies showed just how modeful was a mentality that had "seized control"—particularly the analytical-problem-solving one (which identifies most strongly with the Bruner symbolic mentality). For example, after working on five analytic tasks in a row, if a problem was given that was trivial to solve figuratively, the solver could be blocked for hours trying to solve it symbolically. This makes quite a bit of sense when you consider that the main jobs of the three mentalities are:

**enactive:** know where you are, manipulate

**iconic:** recognize, compare, configure, concrete

**symbolic:** tie together long chains of reasoning, abstract...

Out of all this came the main slogan I coined to express this goal:
*Doing with Images makes Symbols*
The slogan also implies—as did Bruner—that one should start with—be grounded in—the concrete "Doing with Images," and be carried into the more abstract "makes Symbols."

All the ingredients were already around. We were ready to notice what the theoretical frameworks from other fields of Bruner, Gallwey, and others were trying to tell us. What is surprising to me is just how long it took to put it all together. After Xerox PARC provided the opportunity to turn these ideas into reality, it still took our group about five years and experiments with hundreds of users to come up with the first practical design that was in accord with Bruner's model and really worked.

| DOING | mouse | *enactive* | know where you are, manipulate |
|---|---|---|---|
| with IMAGES | icons, windows | *iconic* | recognize, compare, configure, concrete |
| makes SYMBOLS | Smalltalk | *symbolic* | tie together long chains of reasoning, abstract |

Part of the reason perhaps was that the theory was much better at confirming that an idea was good than at actually generating the ideas. In fact, in certain areas like "iconic programming," it actually held back progress, for example, the simple use of icons as signs, because the siren's song of trying to do symbolic thinking iconically was just too strong.

Some of the smaller areas were obvious and found their place in the framework immediately. Probably the most intuitive was the idea of multiple overlapping windows. NLS [oN-Line System] had multiple panes, FLEX had multiple windows, and the bitmap display that we thought was too small, but that was made from individual pixels, led quickly to the idea that windows could appear to overlap. The contrastive ideas of Bruner suggested that there should always be a way to compare. The flitting-about nature of the iconic mentality suggested that having as many resources showing on the screen as possible would be a good way to encourage creativity and problem solving and prevent blockage. An intuitive way to use the windows was to activate the window that the mouse was in and bring it to the "top." This interaction was *modeless* in a special sense of the word. The active window constituted a mode to be sure—one window might hold a painting kit, another might hold text— but one could get to the next window to do something in *without any special termination*. This is what *modeless* came to mean for me—the user could always get to the next thing desired without any backing out. The contrast of the nice modeless interactions of windows with the clumsy command syntax of most previous systems directly suggested that everything should be made modeless. Thus began a campaign to "get rid of modes."

The object-oriented nature of Smalltalk was very suggestive.[4] For example, *object-oriented* means that the object knows what it can do. In the abstract symbolic arena, it means we should first write the object's name (or whatever will fetch it) and then follow with a message it can understand that asks it to do something. In the concrete user-interface arena, it suggests that we should select the object first. It can then furnish us with a menu of what it is willing to do. In both cases we have the *object* first and the desire second. This unifies the concrete with the abstract in a highly satisfying way.

The most difficult area to get to be modeless was a very tiny one, that of elementary text editing. How to get rid of "insert" and "replace" modes that had plagued a decade of editors? Several people arrived at the solution simultaneously. My route came as the result of several beginning-programmer adults who were having trouble building a paragraph editor in Smalltalk, a problem I thought should be easy. Over a weekend I built a sample paragraph editor whose main simplification was that it eliminated the distinction between insert, replace, and delete by allowing selections to extend between the characters. Thus, there could be a zero-width selection, and thus every operation could be a replace. "Insert" meant replace the zero-width selection. "Delete" meant replace the selection with a zero-width string of characters. I got the tiny one-page program running in Smalltalk and came in crowing over the victory. Larry Tesler thought it was great and showed me the idea, already working in his new Gypsy editor (which he implemented on the basis of a suggestion from Peter Deutsch). So much for creativity and invention when ideas are in the air. As Goethe noted, the most important thing is to enjoy the thrill of discovery rather than to make vain attempts to claim priority!...

4 Smalltalk, an early object-oriented programming language, influenced many contemporary languages, including Java, Python, and Ruby.

The only stumbling place for this onrushing braver new world is that all of its marvels will be very difficult to communicate with, because, as always, the user interface design that could make it all simple lags far, far behind. If communication is the watchword, then what do we communicate with and how do we do it?

We communicate with:

• Our selves

• Our tools

• Our colleagues and others

• Our agents

Until now, personal computing has concentrated mostly on the first two. Let us now extend everything we do to be part of a grand collaboration—with one's self, one's tools, other humans, and, increasingly, with agents: computer processes that act as guide, as coach, and as amanuensis. The user interface design will be the critical factor in the success of this new way to work and play on the computer. One of the implications is that the "network" will not be seen at all, but rather "felt" as a shift in capacity and range from that experienced via one's own hard disk....

Well, there are so many more new issues that must be explored as well. I say thank goodness for that. How do we navigate in once-again uncharted waters? I have always believed that of all the ways to approach the future, the vehicle that gets you to the most interesting places is romance. The notion of tool has always been a romantic idea to humankind—from swords to musical instruments to personal computers, it has been easy to say: "The best way to predict the future is to invent it!" The romantic dream of "How nice it would be if…" often has the power to bring the vision to life. Though the notion of management of complex processes has less cachet than that of the hero single-handedly wielding a sword, the real romance of management is nothing less than the creation of civilization itself. What a strange and interesting frontier to investigate. As always, the strongest weapon we have to explore this new world is the one between our ears—providing it's loaded!

**ERIK VAN BLOKLAND AND JUST VAN ROSSUM CHALLENGE DESIGNERS TO PROGRAM THEIR WAY BEYOND THE LIMITATIONS OF OUT-OF-THE-BOX SOFTWARE.** As the two type designers have pointed out, if no program exists to enact what you wish to do, it might just mean that you have a new idea.[1] Van Blokland and van Rossum have collaborated over the years as LettError, a name they came up with while studying graphic design at the Royal Academy of Art in The Hague in the Netherlands. In 1990 Erik Spiekermann released Beowolf, the first LettError typeface, as the inaugural font in his new digital font library FontFont by FontShop. Beowolf, a so-called RandomFont, looked beyond the concept of type as identical mass-produced copies. Instead, using then-cutting-edge PostScript technology, van Blokland and van Rossum pro-grammed the font to take a unique form with each printing, thus demonstrating the shocking dematerialization of type from physical object to a set of instructions. LettError valued this dematerialization, recognizing its potential for revolutionary typographic form, and began experimenting with integrating "programming-assisted design" into their wider methodology. In this approach the designer sets up specific parameters and then asks the computer to randomly vary those parameters, thus quickly producing lots of possible design solutions. LettError continues these explorations today: since the 1990s the firm has produced more than fifty fonts. The commercial success of van Blokland and van Rossum's work speaks to the potential in their assertion that programming is too important to be left to programmers.[2]

1  Erik van Blokland and
   Jan Middendorp, "Tools,"
   in *LettError* (Amsterdam:
   Rosbeek, 2000), 20-30.

2  Ibid.

# IS BEST REALLY BETTER

**ERIK VAN BLOKLAND AND JUST VAN ROSSUM | 1990**

The developments in typeface design, typesetting, and printing have always been aimed at the improvement of "quality." Compared to printing techniques as they existed in the early fifteenth century, we have indeed come a long way. We can digitally output the most perfectly drawn typefaces onto film in resolu-tions of up to five thousand lines per inch. We can print in offset, in perfect registration, on the smoothest papers, and finish it off with layers of varnish, all at a speed that our fifteenth-century forefathers would find baffling. Technically we can create the slickest printing ever, reach the highest possible quality ever. Unfortunately, the results have too often become absolutely boring. The quality of a printed product, the high resolution of its typefaces, the perfect printing are not necessarily what makes for good design or clear communication.

As a reaction to this development, we decided to create a typeface that would add liveliness to the page that has since long been lost using the modern technologies available.

Our typeface would have a high-resolution distortion of its digital outlines with lengthy rasterizing times as opposed to most developments in digital type: the unsmooth and slow versus the slick and quick.

Type has always been in flux. Gutenberg started with whole copied pages cut from a single piece of wood. All the characters were hand-cut and no two a's were the same. And did anyone mind? Gutenberg imitated handwriting because it was the only model of letterforms available at that time. He simply developed a process that was already there, but he succeeded in doing it faster. Only later were the advantages of movable type exploited, when hot metal type casting techniques made it possible to create large quantities of type in a relatively inexpensive fashion. This was also the period when letterforms started taking advantage of this new medium. [Giambattista] Bodoni cut serifs so thin that it would have been impossible to produce them out of wood. It has always taken a while for people to realize the potential of a new technology.

Today's fonts work the way they do because they are still created in a hot metal, movable type kind of way. Their design is based upon the process of punch cutting, which creates a matrix from which an infinite number of identical copies of each letter can be made. Digital type may even "crash" just as hot metal typesetting did. And, ironically, digital type has resulted in a revival of old style and non-lining numerals and even small caps. The usage of type is still based upon the proverbial type cases that were divided into different compartments, each for a different letter. When a certain letter is needed, it is put in line with the others to make words and sentences. Today the type case is replaced by a font and a digital printer.

Through our experience with traditional typesetting methods, we have come to expect that the individual letterforms of a particular typeface should always look the same. This notion is the result of a technical process, not the other way around. However, there is no technical reason for making a digital letter the same every time it is printed. It is possible to calculate every point and every curve differently each time the letter is generated by slightly moving the points that define a character in various "random" directions. We discovered that it was possible to create a font featuring these characteristics in PostScript; our result was Beowolf, the first RandomFont typeface of its kind. (Actually, [Donald] Knuth got there first, and he was nice about it.)

Random technology, which is what we call the programming that is involved, is about letting the rasterizer behave randomly within the boundaries of legibility. Instead of re-creating a fixed outline or bitmap, the RandomFont redefines its outlines every time they are called for. Thus, each character will be different each time it is printed. All the points that define the outline of any character will be nudged in a random direction. The distance moved depends on the parameters. For instance, Beowolf 21 has a little deviation, Beowolf 22 has a noticeable wrinkle, and Beowolf 23 is definitely mad.

What is interesting about this typeface is that the deviations in the individual letterforms create an overall unity, and the liveliness of the page that we were after is accomplished. We also discovered an interesting side effect when creating color separations for four-color printing. Since the printer (Linotronic in this case) generates different outlines each time it prints a particular letter, the color separation will result in four different nonmatching films. The resulting letterform in print will be outlined in bright colors.

While working on RandomFont, we became aware that if we treated typefaces as computer data instead of fixed letterforms, we could create some very bizarre systems. One idea was to connect a font file to a self-copying moving mechanism to create a virus font; a self-distributing typeface: a great way for young and ambitious type designers to get their typefaces known and used. No type manufacturer would be able to compete with that kind of immediate proliferation. Or we could change typographic awareness of computer users around the world by creating a font virus that would transform every Helvetica into something much more desirable—the postmodern typographer's revenge. Virowolves that travel around the world in a single day, with type designers getting paid by buying network shares. Or we could hand out our fonts at conferences and meetings, but after a while the files will turn sour just like milk. A perfectly good font would turn random over time. A great way to force people to eventually buy a legitimate copy. And you better hurry, or the virus font will affect your other fonts as well!

We could release a typeface that deteriorates over time, slowly turning into a Beowolf-like face, scaring the hell out of its users. We could create letters that wear out through frequent use, combined with a feature that uses up certain often-used letters. You want real letterpress quality? You can get it! How about a font that adds typos? Link a number of typos to a particular time of the day and simulate an erratic (human) typesetter or a font that does not work overtime.

If we put more data into our typefaces, we can have some very intelligent fonts. Some applications could be quite practical. For instance, the data could include the information to create automatic ink traps that would switch on or off automatically, or as specified by the user, depending on the size of the type or printing technique used. A font would modify its outline when it is to be printed in offset, or shown on TV, or screened on wood, or whatever. Or a typeface could research weather data, in particular the amount of direct sunlight on the spot where it will be printed, and modify itself to the best possible contrast.

The idea of RandomFont can be applied elsewhere too. Why should a letterhead always be the same? It can be slightly different each day. If you print your correspondence or invoices on a LaserWriter, you can have a random logo, a logo that changes itself, moves around the page, or tells something interesting about your company, the person you are writing to, or the nature of the letter. The dynamic logo can be much more informative than its fixed alternative.

For years graphic designers, especially those who subscribe to the ideas and philosophies of Swiss design or modernism, have argued that logos and typefaces should appear consistent to establish recognition. We don't think that this is necessary. Creating a random logo for a company, with letterheads and forms on which the logo would move around and change, does not necessarily decrease recognizability. Recognition does not come from simple repetition of the same form but is something much more intelligent, something that happens in our minds. When you hear somebody's voice on the phone and he or she has a cold, you can still recognize who is talking. We can recognize handwriting and even decipher how quickly a note was written and sometimes pick up on the state of mind the person was in when writing the note. Randomness and change can add new dimensions to print work.

Randomness within typography is not a revolutionary idea either. Typographers have always had to deal with randomness because type has always lacked standardization and consistency. One example is the measurement of type. With hot metal type everybody measured the body size of a typeface. With phototype and digital type there is no body to be measured. Some people like to measure the x-height, others the cap-height. Even the computer industry has added to the confusion. Software developers in different countries have each taken their national typographic standards and type measurement units and have written programs using their respective systems. This becomes a problem when, for instance, software written by an American developer is sold in Europe and the user must switch to the American measurement system.

There are software programs that will interpret between the various existing measurement systems, but the conversions are performed internally. So two centimeters will inevitably output as 2.0001 or 1.9999 centimeters; it never works precisely. Randomness will always exist. There is definitely not going to be a universal set of standards for type and typography. Maybe randomness is an inevitable result of human behavior. Gutenberg's letters came out looking slightly different each time they were printed. Letters wore out, some got damaged, the impression onto the paper differed. However, overall the printed results had a vibrant and human quality. At some point during the development of type and typography, the graphic design industry decided that is was necessary to improve upon the "quality" of printing and type. In the process, due to economic and commercial considerations, much vitality was lost. We believe that the computer, although considered by many to be cold and impersonal, can bring back some of these lost qualities. RandomFont is our contribution to this idea.

IN ANY CREATIVE DISCIPLINE, THE TOOLS INFLUENCE THE PROCESS AND, INDIRECTLY, THE RESULTS. WE TRY TO BE AWARE OF THIS INFLUENCE, AND IF IT IS SOMETHING WE DON'T LIKE, WE TRY TO CHANGE IT.

ERIK VAN BLOKLAND
Interview in *Processing*
2007

**IN THE MID-1980S, DESIGNER P. SCOTT MAKELA TOOK THE ADVICE OF APRIL GREIMAN AND BOUGHT A MAC. HE NEVER LOOKED BACK.** His fervent, chaotic work—so unlike the then-pervasive Swiss style design—gained the respect of older design luminaries, although his style was strikingly not to their taste. Makela did not even spare the sanctity of typographic tradition. To create Dead History, a typeface for Emigre Fonts, he spliced together two existing digital typefaces, Linotype Centennial and Adobe VAG Rounded, with no care for elegance or precision. In his influential projects, such as the video for Michael Jackson's song "Scream" and film title sequences, particularly that of *Fight Club*, Makela used technology to flood the senses with a shocking multimedia experience, thereby defining the postmodern aesthetic of the early 1990s. His mantra was, "It must bleed on all four sides."[1] With his wife, Laurie Haycock—a design force in her own right— he codirected the influential Cranbrook Academy of Art's graphic design program. Together this power couple taught students to look to their own private obsessions as an impetus for design practice.[2]

1  Michael Rock, "P. Scott Makela Is Wired," *Eye* 12 (spring 1994): 26–35.

2  Makela died at age thirty-nine from a rare infection of the epiglottis.

# REDEFINING DISPLAY

### P. SCOTT MAKELA | 1993

Father Richard LaCosse is the only priest in his rectory with a computer work wall in his room. There, a large, periscope-projection fabric screen flickers with video patches as the transparent digital pages of books overlap. Several colleagues call him on the videophone; their images can be adjusted in size and by proximity to each other. LaCosse's research is interrupted by the appearance of a drawn red curtain at the left of his screen. The online confession that then begins shares the electronic screen space with his other daily work but is appropriately darkened and isolated.

This is just one fantasy for a new kind of electronic office, in which signals will be clearer, stronger, and more realistic than ever. With the application of optimal broadband fiber optics and the aggressive programming of television, personal computers, and telephones, systems like Father LaCosse's may be available late in this decade. As the techno-hip wait for workable, day-to-day access to the three-dimensional computer simulation called virtual reality, they will continue to devise new ways of framing information on the screen. After the complete digital submergence promised by VR has been achieved, our ways of planning and executing work, communications, rituals, and leisure activities will never be the same. Until then, though, how do we choose the programming and delivery of our daily electronic stuff? Surely the current screen icons of file folders, trash cans, and windows are stiff and limiting. New paradigms for these digital presentations are needed to augment the spatial experience and optical excitement that the VR goggles, gloves, and suits have promised to deliver.

If we could dispense with the conventional office as the major metaphor for our computer visuals, we would be better able to represent our minds' memories, dreams, and visions. We have begun by loosening the formats and softening the presentation of data, but everyone has a different idea of what such departures mean. Some people might use the screen to frame the pleasant confusion of the daily work routine; to many of us the messy desk is a useful structure. Others might arrange their media information and output on the screen with the pragmatism and care used by a biologist preparing a culture specimen. Flexibility in forming personal-data terrains and textures is sure to help make our workstations warmer and more comfortable than they are now.

Awareness of my own working methods has helped me to visualize others' data-processing needs. Every day I make multiple phone calls while my Macintosh runs up to six software programs at once. I send faxes and email, and I am productively addicted to good electronic bulletin boards. I watch obscure satellite TV stations…, and I enjoy CDs played at high volume. Soon, when new hardware permits, I hope to add to this mix the capacity to make instant, simultaneous, high-resolution image and text transfers between terminals. I want to conduct seamless multiple-videophone conversations…and to acquire a larger on-screen working area. If only I could arrange and mold the electronic information that appears before me in the same way I unconsciously compose my desk. Depictions of the contents of my pockets…would share the screen with my software applications, vacation photos, pages from books, and stills from CNN. These images, though digital, would accurately portray the idiosyncratic elements of my daily life.

The models illustrated (realized with the help of Alex) here [see p. 94] are my subjective forecasts of how individual work walls might appear to a parish priest, an artist, a motorcycle mechanic, and a plumber, whose needs and notions of order define their digital working and communication spaces. For example, the priest conducts a primary conversation with one person whose likeness appears in full scale. Text that relates to a current conversation falls directly over an on-screen face. The artist uses online services that help him select and join various media in his work. A caller's face is contained in a small soft circle in the upper left corner, an image inspired by signers for the hearing-impaired on Sunday morning TV religious services. The motorcycle mechanic chooses to mass her visuals, business documents, and current projects on one side of the screen, while on the other side she focuses on the precise details of a pipe cutter. The plumber prefers large background images of his upcoming fishing vacation. He files through old invoices, fittings, and valve diagrams. His grandchild links in to say hello, just as an angry client calls. Though the digital office will never completely replace the physical one, the signals we send and receive ought to better mirror the experiences and dramas of each user's daily existence.

**JOHN MAEDA UNCOILS THE POTENTIAL OF COMPUTATION AND AESTHETICS, DEMONSTRAT-ING AGAIN AND AGAIN THAT THESE TWO DISCIPLINES CAN AND WILL FEED ONE ANOTHER IN THE DECADES TO COME.** A meticulous sense of craft and labor—both of which Maeda learned growing up in his father's tofu store—coupled with study in engineering, computer science, art, and design produced this innovative leader. In the mid-1990s, he founded the Aesthetics and Computation Group at the MIT Media Lab (ACG). There, brilliant minds experimented with raw computation as a unique expressive medium. Influential students, including Casey Reas, Ben Fry, Golan Levin, Peter Cho, and Reed Kram, helped spread the confluence of design and code through their work. In the years following Maeda's thirteen-year stint at ACG, he served as president of the Rhode Island School of Design. He is currently a partner at Kleiner Perkins Caufield & Byers and chairs the eBay Design Advisory Council. In these roles, Maeda continues to advocate for the centrality of art and design within the technological framework of our lives.

# DESIGN BY NUMBERS

**JOHN MAEDA | 1999**

Drawing by hand, using pencil on paper, is undisputedly the most natural means for visual expression. When moving on to the world of digital expression, however, the most natural means is not pencil and paper but, rather, computation. Today, many people strive to combine the traditional arts with the computer; and while they may succeed at producing a digitally empowered version of their art, they are not producing true digital art. True digital art embodies the core characteristics of the digital medium, which cannot be replicated in any other.

Computation is intrinsically different from existing media because it is the only medium where the material and the process for shaping the material coexist in the same entity: numbers. The only other medium where a similar phenomenon occurs is pure thought. It naturally follows that computational media could eventually present the rare opportunity to express a conceptual art that is not polluted by textual or other visual representation. This exciting future is still at least a decade or two away. For the moment, we are forced to settle with society's current search for true meaning in an enhanced, interactive version of the art that we have always known.

ABCDEFGHIJK
LMNOPQRSTUV
WXYZabcdefgh
ijklmnopqrstuvx
xyz0123456789
ÆŒœŒfifl!?&@*
¢$¥£¶%™©®†#
()[]{}''""'';:.,

**P. SCOTT MAKELA** Dead History
typeface, Emigre Fonts, 1990.

**APRIL GREIMAN** *Snow White + the Seven Pixels, An Evening with April Greiman,* 1986, poster for a presentation at the Maryland Institute College of Art in Baltimore. Greiman studied under Armin Hofmann and Wolfgang Weingart at the Schule für Gestaltung Basel in Switzerland. Her work in the 1980s is synonymous with New Wave design in the United States. She enthusiastically used computers during a time when many designers either dismissed such technology as useless or were frightened by what it would mean for design craft.

*clockwise from top left:* **MURIEL COOPER** *Self-portrait with Polaroid SX-70,* video imaged and printed at the Visible Language Workshop, MIT, ca. 1982.

**MURIEL COOPER AND RON MACNEIL** Messages and Means course poster, designed and printed at the Visible Language Workshop, MIT, ca. 1974.

**MURIEL COOPER WITH DAVID SMALL, SUGURU ISHIZAKI, AND LISA STRAUSFELD** Still from *Information Landscapes,* 1994.

Influenced by avant-garde workshop structures and Bauhaus luminaries– Walter Gropius and György Kepes were in Cambridge at the time– Cooper thoroughly explored and resisted methodologies born of mass production and mass communication. In a rumpled sweater, old glasses, and bare feet, she swept into the male-dominated MIT Media Lab and redefined the screen as a nonlinear information environment.

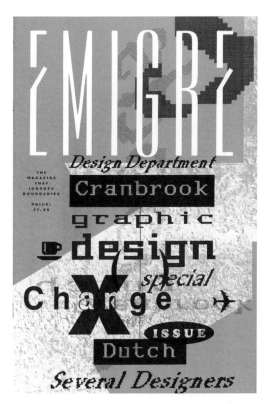

**GRADUATE STUDENTS AT CRANBROOK ACADEMY OF ART** *Emigre* 10, 1988. This student-designed issue of *Emigre* explores an exchange program between Cranbrook students and Dutch graphic design studios. Under the leadership of Katherine McCoy, Cranbrook was at the time a hotbed of postmodern thinking.

**RUDY VANDERLANS** *Emigre* 11, "Ambition/Fear," 1989. This issue of *Emigre* gathers responses from graphic designers to the newly introduced Macintosh. In the layout, VanderLans, inspired by the pairing of typefaces with characters in Warren Lehrer's book *French Fries*, assigns a unique typeface to each interview. The resulting dense, interwoven layout suggests the excitement then felt by the design world about the personal computer.

ABCDEFGHIJKL
MNOPQRSTUV
WXYZabcdefgh
ijklmnopqrst
uvwxyz
0123456789
ÆŒœæ!?&@*
¢$¥£€%‰™©®†#
()[]{}"'""‚·.,

**ZUZANA LICKO** Oakland, 1985. Licko created the bitmap type designs Emperor, Oakland, and Emigre for the coarse resolutions of 1980s computer screens and the dot-matrix printer. Rather than resisting the computer's limitations, she used them to generate unexpected forms appropriate to the technology. Licko first used her typefaces in *Emigre* 2 and began running ads for them in issue 3. In 1985 Licko and Rudy VanderLans launched Emigre Fonts.

# USER A:

**ANDREW** ... MULTIMEDIA ARTIST
AND AN EDITOR OF PUBLIC ACCESS DATA
FOR VARIOUS INTERNATIONAL IMAGE
BANKS AND DATA GROUPS. HIS IS A
WORLD OF CONSTANT COMMUNICATION
WITH COLLEAGUES AND NEW FRIENDS.

HE OFTEN TOOK ...

ANDREW IS ... FINICKY ...
THE ORDER ... HIERARCHY ...

TWO OF HIS FRIENDS HAVE CALLED ...
MINUTES APART AND HE TALKS TO EACH

POLY(though)

HARLEY-DAVIDSON

Dear Tiger,
The new glass-packs are
fabulous. Coming out on the
road next week with the
bale. I will bring materials
from the vintage ... show ...
in Montreal.

Best regards,

# USER B:

**CLAIRE** IS A MOTORCYCLE MECHANIC
WHO SPECIALIZES IN VINTAGE AMERICAN
MACHINES. SHE RESPONDS TO A LOOSE
AND MESSY ... AND HAS ALWAYS ...
TEN PROJECTS AT ONCE.

RETRACT    BANKS    WRITE

OMNI

BCAST

DESCRIPTIONS OF REPAIR PROJECTS IN
HER SHOP ARE SCANNED INTO THE
SYSTEM SO THAT ON-LINE SOURCES OF
PARTS AND SERVICE CAN BE FOUND.

VIEWS OF UTAH FILL THE BACKGROUND
AS CLAIRE ANTICIPATES HER VACATION.

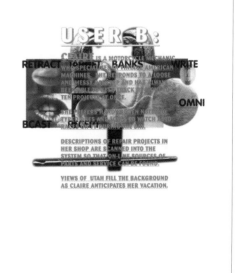

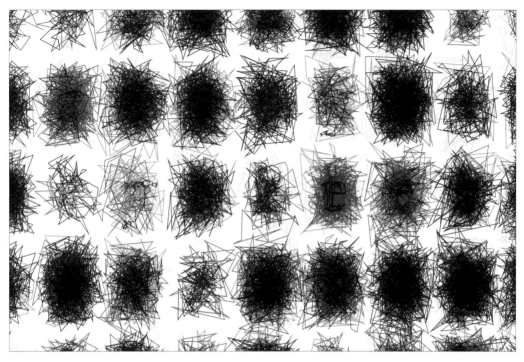

*opposite:* **P. SCOTT MAKELA**
Illustrations from "Redefining
Display," 1993, showing a parish
priest, an artist, a motorcycle
mechanic, and a plumber: Here,
Makela urges his audience to move
away from boxes and grids to a
wild, chaotic place of overlapping
planes where everything happens
simultaneously.

*above:* **ERIK VAN BLOKLAND
AND JUST VAN ROSSUM OF
LETTERROR** Beowolf, 1989. Van
Blokland and van Rossum initially
proposed the concept of Random-
Fonts in their first and only issue
of *LettError* magazine. The idea
came out of their experiments
with then-cutting-edge PostScript
technology. RandomFonts morphed
into Beowolf as the two designers
played around with programmed
randomness to add imperfection
to slick computer imagery.

# ENCODING THE FUTURE

**AS THE NEW MILLENNIUM BEGAN, SOCIAL MEDIA PROLIFERATED. ALTHOUGH ITS ROOTS GO BACK TO THE LATE TWENTIETH CENTURY— WHICH SAW THE INVENTION OF THE WHOLE EARTH 'LECTRONIC LINK, THE WORLD WIDE WEB, AOL INSTANT MESSENGER, GOOGLE, AND BLOGGER—WIDESPREAD USE OF SOCIAL MEDIA AS AN IMPETUS FOR CONVERSATION AND COLLABORATION DID NOT TAKE OFF UNTIL THE EARLY 2000s.** Designers such as Khoi Vinh and Hugh Dubberly paid close attention as communication transformed from a one-to-many broadcast model to a many-to-many platform, and began to relinquish modernist tenets of control and precision, opting instead to develop systems that guide user behavior and content. Collectives such as Conditional Design worked not just to put systems into play but also to watch those systems take on lives of their own. Collaborative making and iterative testing became a model for software developers *and* designers. The exponential increase in computing power suddenly made complexity feasible, allow-ing designers to emulate organic, generative approaches. Casey Reas and Ben Fry, building on the work of John Maeda and Muriel Cooper, celebrated software as a new aesthetic with the release of Processing. Using tools such as Arduino, creatives began to experiment with distributed sensor networks to engage with big data and, when possible, get closer to the natural ecosystems surrounding us. Futurists looked beyond smart objects to consider the design needs of a posthuman world— a world dominated by hybrid human/machine intelligence. Such seismic shifts in the profession force designers to pause and take stock of their identity as designers and humans—that is, if they can take the time to catch their breath.

**ARDUINO** The Arduino company produces inexpensive micro-controller boards with an integrated development language that allows users to connect their devices to the environment through sensors and actuators. Arduino developed its open-source platform as an offshoot of Processing in 2005. Its endeavors provided an early step toward the Internet of Things (IoT).

**BEN FRY AND CASEY REAS REPRESENT A NEW BREED OF DESIGNER/ARTIST/PROGRAMMER.**
While graduate students in John Maeda's Aesthetics and Computation Group at the MIT Media Lab, Fry and Reas began working on a project that we now know as Processing. In 2001 they released this open-source language and environment, thereby luring creatives into computation and technologists into aesthetic experimentation.[1] Inspired by Muriel Cooper's Visual Language Workshop and Maeda's Design by Numbers project, Fry and Reas actualized dreams of bridging art and technology passionately pursued by so many over the last century, including members of the Bauhaus in the 1920s and the New Tendencies and Op Art movements in the 1960s. Thousands upon thousands of artists, designers, and programmers responded and continue to respond to Processing's free and open-source structure by downloading, using, expanding, and improving it. And the influence of this evolving language and environment does not stop there. Processing's legacy includes equally powerful artistic tools, such as Arduino, a platform enabling the integration of electronics into creative practice.[2] Processing and its children break down the wall between art and technology with the lasting blows of a sledgehammer.

1 "Overview," Processing, April 30, 2015, https://processing.org/overview/.

2 For more about Arduino and its predecessor, Wiring, see Daniel Shiffman, "Interview with Casey Reas and Ben Fry," *Rhizome*, September 23, 2009, http://rhizome.org/editorial/2009/sep/23/interview-with-casey-reas-and-ben-fry/.

# PROCESSING...

**BEN FRY AND CASEY REAS | 2007**

Processing relates software concepts to principles of visual form, motion, and interaction. It integrates a programming language, development environment, and teaching methodology into a unified system. Processing was created to teach fundamentals of computer programming within a visual context, to serve as a software sketchbook, and to be used as a production tool. Students, artists, design professionals, and researchers use it for learning, prototyping, and production.

The Processing language is a text programming language specifically designed to generate and modify images. Processing strives to achieve a balance between clarity and advanced features. Beginners can write their own programs after only a few minutes of instruction, but more advanced users can employ and write libraries with additional functions. The system facilitates teaching many computer graphics and interaction techniques, including vector/raster drawing, image processing, color models, mouse and keyboard events, network communication, and object-oriented programming. Libraries easily extend Processing's ability to generate sound, send/receive data in diverse formats, and to import/export 2-D and 3-D file formats.

## SOFTWARE

A group of beliefs about the software medium set the conceptual foundation for Processing and inform decisions related to designing the software and environment.

*Software is a unique medium with unique qualities.*
Concepts and emotions that are not possible to express in other media may be expressed in this medium. Software requires its own terminology and discourse and should not be evaluated in relation to prior media such as film, photography, and painting. History shows that technologies such as oil paint, cameras, and film have changed artistic practice and discourse, and while we do not claim that new technologies improve art, we do feel they enable different forms of communication and expression. Software holds a unique position among artistic media because of its ability to produce dynamic forms, process gestures, define behavior, simulate natural systems, and integrate other media, including sound, image, and text.

*Every programming language is a distinct material.*
As with any medium, different materials are appropriate for different tasks. When designing a chair, a designer decides to use steel, wood, or other materials based on the intended use and on personal ideas and tastes. This scenario transfers to writing software. The abstract animator and programmer Larry Cuba describes his experience this way: "Each of my films has been made on a different system using a different programming language. A programming language gives you the power to express some ideas, while limiting your abilities to express others."[3] There are many programming languages available from which to choose, and some are more appropriate than others depending on the project goals. The Processing language utilizes a common computer programming syntax that makes it easy for people to extend the knowledge gained through its use to many diverse programming languages.

*Sketching is necessary for the development of ideas.*
It is necessary to sketch in a medium related to the final medium so the sketch can approximate the finished product. Painters may construct elaborate drawings and sketches before executing the final work. Architects traditionally work first in cardboard and wood to better understand their forms in space. Musicians often work with a piano before scoring a more complex composition. To sketch electronic media, it's important to work with electronic materials. Just as each programming language is a distinct material, some are better for sketching than others, and artists working in

3 Larry Cuba, "Calculated Movements," in *Prix Ars Electronica Edition '87: Meisterwerke der Computerkunst* (H. S. Sauer, 1987), 111.

software need environments for working through their ideas before writing final code. Processing is built to act as a software sketchbook, making it easy to explore and refine many different ideas within a short period of time.

*Programming is not just for engineers.*

Many people think programming is only for people who are good at math and other technical disciplines. One reason programming remains within the domain of this type of personality is that the technically minded people usually create programming languages. It is possible to create different kinds of programming languages and environments that engage people with visual and spatial minds. Alternative languages such as Processing extend the programming space to people who think differently. An early alternative language was Logo, designed in the late 1960s by Seymour Papert as a language concept for children. Logo made it possible for children to program many different media, including a robotic turtle and graphic images on-screen. A more contemporary example is the Max programming environment developed by Miller Puckette in the 1980s. Max is different from typical languages; its programs are created by connecting boxes that represent the program code, rather than lines of text. It has generated enthusiasm from thousands of musicians and visual artists who use it as a base for creating audio and visual software. The same way graphical user interfaces opened up computing for millions of people, alternative programming environments will continue to enable new generations of artists and designers to work directly with software. We hope Processing will encourage many artists and designers to tackle software and that it will stimulate interest in other programming environments built for the arts.

## LITERACY

Processing does not present a radical departure from the current culture of programming. It repositions programming in a way that is accessible to people who are interested in programming but who may be intimidated by or uninterested in the type taught in computer science departments. The computer originated as a tool for fast calculations and has evolved into a medium for expression.

The idea of general software literacy has been discussed since the early 1970s. In 1974 Ted Nelson wrote about the minicomputers of the time in *Computer Lib/Dream Machines*. He explained, "The more you know about computers...the better your imagination can flow between the

4 Theodore Nelson, "Computer Lib/Dream Machines," in *The New Media Reader,* edited by Noah Wardrip-Fruin and Nick Montfort (MIT Press, 2003), 306.

technicalities, can slide the parts together, can discern the shapes of what you would have these things do."[4] In his book, Nelson discusses potential futures for the computer as a media tool and clearly outlines ideas for hypertexts (linked text, which set the foundation for the Web) and hypergrams (interactive drawings). Developments at Xerox PARC led to the Dynabook, a prototype for today's personal computers. The Dynabook vision included more than hardware. A programming language was written to enable, for example, children to write storytelling and drawing programs and musicians to write composition programs. In this vision there was no distinction between a computer user and a programmer.

Thirty years after these optimistic ideas, we find ourselves in a different place. A technical and cultural revolution did occur through the introduction of the personal computer and the Internet to a wider audience, but people are overwhelmingly using the software tools created by professional programmers rather than making their own. This situation is described clearly by John Maeda in his book *Creative Code:* "To use a tool on a computer, you need do little more than point and click; to create a tool, you must understand the arcane art of computer programming."[5] The negative aspects of this situation are the constraints imposed by software tools. As a result of being easy to use, these tools obscure some of the computer's potential. To fully explore the computer as an artistic material, it's important to understand this "arcane art of computer programming."

5 John Maeda, *Creative Code* (Thames & Hudson, 2004), 113.

Processing strives to make it possible and advantageous for people within the visual arts to learn how to build their own tools—to become software literate. Alan Kay, a pioneer at Xerox PARC and Apple, explains what literacy means in relation to software: "The ability to 'read' a medium means you can access materials and tools created by others. The ability to 'write' in a medium means you can generate materials and tools for others. You must have both to be literate. In print writing, the tools you generate are rhetorical; they demonstrate and convince. In computer writing, the tools you generate are processes; they simulate and decide."[6] Making processes that simulate and decide requires programming.

6 Alan Kay, "User Interface: A Personal View," in *The Art of Human-Computer Interface Design,* edited by Brenda Laurel (Addison-Wesley, 1989), 193.

## OPEN

The open source software movement is having a major impact on our culture and economy through initiatives such as Linux, but it is having a smaller influence on the culture surrounding software for the arts. There are scattered small projects, but companies such as Adobe and Microsoft dominate software production and therefore control the future of software tools used within the arts. As a group, artists and designers traditionally lack the technical skills to support independent software initiatives. Processing strives to apply the spirit of open source software innovation to the domain of the arts. We want to provide an alternative to available proprietary software and to improve the skills of the arts community, thereby stimulating interest in related initiatives. We want to make Processing easy to extend and adapt and to make it available to as many people as possible.

Processing probably would not exist without its ties to open source software. Using existing open source projects as guidance, and for important software components, has allowed the project to develop in a smaller amount of time and without a large team of programmers. Individuals are more likely to donate their time to an open source project, and therefore the software evolves without a budget. These factors allow the software to be distributed without cost, which enables access to people who cannot afford the high prices of commercial software. The Processing source code allows people to learn from its construction and by extending it with their own code.

People are encouraged to publish the code for programs they've written in Processing. The same way the "view source" function in Web browsers encouraged the rapid proliferation of website-creation skills, access to others' Processing code enables members of the community to learn from each other so that the skills of the community increase as a whole. A good example involves writing software for tracking objects in a video image, thus allowing people to interact directly with the software through their bodies, rather than through a mouse or keyboard. The original submitted code worked well but was limited to tracking only the brightest object in the frame. Karsten Schmidt (aka toxi), a more experienced programmer, used this code as a foundation for writing more general code that could track multiple colored objects at the same time. Using this improved tracking code as infrastructure enabled Laura Hernandez Andrade, a graduate student at UCLA, to build Talking Colors, an interactive installation that superimposes emotive text about the colors people are wearing on top of their projected image. Sharing and improving code allows people to learn from one another and to build projects that would be too complex to accomplish without assistance.

## EDUCATION

Processing makes it possible to introduce software concepts in the context of the arts and also to open arts concepts to a more technical audience. Because the Processing syntax is derived from widely used programming languages, it's a good base for future learning. Skills learned with Processing enable people to learn other programming languages suitable for different contexts, including Web authoring, networking, electronics, and computer graphics.

There are many established curricula for computer science, but by comparison there have been very few classes that strive to integrate media arts knowledge with core concepts of computation. Using classes initiated by John Maeda as a model, hybrid courses based on Processing are being created. Processing has proved useful for short workshops ranging from one day to a few weeks. Because the environment is so minimal, students are able to begin programming after only a few minutes of instruction. The Processing syntax, similar to other common languages, is already familiar to many people, and so students with more experience can begin writing advanced syntax almost immediately....

## NETWORK

Processing takes advantage of the strengths of Web-based communities, and this has allowed the project to grow in unexpected ways. Thousands of students, educators, and practitioners across five continents are involved in using the software. The project website serves as the communication hub, but contributors are found remotely in cities around the world. Typical Web applications such as bulletin boards host discussions between people in remote locations about features, bugs, and related events.

Processing programs are easily exported to the Web, which supports networked collaboration and individuals sharing their work. Many talented people have been learning rapidly and publishing their work, thus inspiring others. Websites such as Jared Tarbell's Complexification.net and Robert Hodgin's Flight404.com present explorations into form, motion, and interaction created in Processing. Tarbell creates images from known algorithms such as Henon Phase diagrams and invents his own algorithms for image creation, such as those from Substrate, which are reminiscent of urban patterns.... On sharing his code from his website, Tarbell writes, "Opening one's code is a beneficial practice for both the programmer and

7 Jared Tarbell, Complexification.net (2004), http://www.complexification.net/medium.html.

the community. I appreciate modifications and extensions of these algorithms."[7] Hodgin is a self-trained programmer who uses Processing to explore the software medium. It has allowed him to move deeper into the topic of simulating natural forms and motion than he could in other programming environments, while still providing the ability to upload his software to the Internet. His highly trafficked website documents these explorations by displaying the running software as well as providing supplemental text, images, and movies. Websites such as those developed by Tarbell and Hodgin are popular destinations for younger artists and designers and other interested individuals. By publishing their work on the Web in this manner, they gain recognition within the community.

Many classes taught using Processing publish the complete curriculum on the Web, and students publish their software assignments and source code, from which others can learn. The websites for Daniel Shiffman's classes at New York University, for example, include online tutorials and links to the students' work. The tutorials for his Procedural Painting course cover topics including modular programming, image processing, and 3-D graphics by combining text with running software examples. Each student maintains a webpage containing all of their software and source code created for the class. These pages provide a straightforward way to review performance and make it easy for members of the class to access each other's work.

The Processing website, www.processing.org, is a place for people to discuss their projects and share advice. The Processing Discourse section of the website, an online bulletin board, has thousands of members, with a subset actively commenting on each other's work and helping with technical questions. For example, a recent post focused on a problem with code to simulate springs. Over the course of a few days, messages were posted discussing the details of Euler integration in comparison to the Runge-Kutta method. While this may sound like an arcane discussion, the differences between the two methods can be the reason a project works well or fails. This thread and many others like it are becoming concise Internet resources for students interested in detailed topics.

**CONTEXT**

The Processing approach to programming blends with established methods. The core language and additional libraries make use of Java, which also has elements identical to the C programming language. This heritage allows

THE BIG IDEA OF PROCESSING IS THE TIGHT INTEGRATION OF A PROGRAMMING ENVIRONMENT, A PROGRAMMING LANGUAGE, A COMMUNITY-MINDED AND OPEN SOURCE MENTALITY, AND A FOCUS ON LEARNING—CREATED BY ARTISTS AND DESIGNERS FOR THEIR OWN COMMUNITY.

CASEY REAS
Interview with
Daniel Shiffman
in *Rhizome*
2009

Processing to make use of decades of programming language refinements and makes it understandable to many people who are already familiar with writing software.

Processing is unique in its emphasis and in the tactical decisions it embodies with respect to its context within design and the arts. Processing makes it easy to write software for drawing, animation, and reacting to the environment, and programs are easily extended to integrate with additional media types, including audio, video, and electronics. Modified versions of the Processing environment have been built by community members to enable programs to run on mobile phones…and to program microcontrollers.…

The network of people and schools using the software continues to grow. In the five years since the origin of the idea for the software, it has evolved organically through presentations, workshops, classes, and discussions around the globe. We plan to continually improve the software and foster its growth with the hope that the practice of programming will reveal its potential as the foundation for a more dynamic media.

LIKE AN ORACLE, PAOLA ANTONELLI SPREADS CLUES BEFORE US. She curates rich, complex museum experiences that encourage participants to themselves construct the present and future of design. Because her exhibitions tend to delve into the current moment, they intersect sharply with technology. The Museum of Modern Art in New York hired the Italian-born Antonelli as a curator in 1994. From the beginning she acted on her instincts. Understanding the communicative power of the Internet, she designed MoMA's first website for her 1995 show *Mutant Materials in Contemporary Design*. Using $300 provided by the museum, she took HTML classes at the School of Visual Arts (SVA) so she could code it herself. Since then she has fearlessly plowed through the snobbery of the art world to seize upon the definitive artifacts and interactions of our time. In 2011 she acquired key video games for the collection: not just the consumer faces of the games, but, when possible, the code itself. Later she challenged the nature of acquisition by bringing to the collection public domain items, including the "@" symbol and Google's pin icon.[1] In 2012 she added to her role as senior curator by founding the museum's Research and Development department, giving formal structure to the think-tank mentality that fuels her endeavors. Rapid manufacturing, mapping, tagging, networked objects, and biodesign are just some of the subjects she tackles; we engage with her exhibition content to better understand the time we live in, a time in which Antonelli finds "designers on top."[2]

1 To learn more about these acquisitions, see "Why I Brought Pac-Man to MoMA," *TED*, May 2013, http://www.ted.com/talks/paola_antonelli_why_i_brought_pacman_to_moma.

2 See Paola Antonelli, "Designers on Top," Eyeo (lecture, Minneapolis, June 5, 2012), https://vimeo.com/44467955.

# DESIGN AND THE ELASTIC MIND

**PAOLA ANTONELLI | 2008**

### DESIGN 1:1

Today, many designers have turned several late-twentieth-century infatuations on their heads, for instance with speed, dematerialization, miniaturization, and a romantic and exaggerated formal expression of complexity. After all, there is a limit beyond which micro-keyboards are too small for a person's fingers and complexity simply becomes too overwhelming. Examples abound in all fields of people's desire to return to what is perceived as a human dimension, including gastronomy (the Slow Food movement), agriculture (organic produce), travel (ecotourism), production of energy (distributed generation), economic aid (microinvestment), and politics (the town hall meeting), to name just a few.[3] These all revolve around the idea that global issues should be tackled bottom up and that an individual or local spark can start a powerful chain reaction with global implications.

3 The Slow Food movement was launched in Italy in 1986 to restore the pleasure of "real" food. It was so successful that it contributed to the "slow" concept now spreading to all dimensions of life, from cities to schools and even to money.

The most contemporary of design theory is devoted to the quest for an environment, whether virtual or physical, built in human proportion—much the way in architecture a hypothetical one-to-one model would represent buildings as life-size. Designers who believe in this preach simplicity, and they

4 Graphic designer and computer scientist John Maeda, who is also associate director of research at the MIT Media Lab, has translated his commitment to the ease of communication between people and objects into a full-fledged platform based on simplicity that involves the Media Lab as well as corporations like the Dutch electronics giant Philips. In this same vein, James Surowiecki's May 28, 2007, article in the *New Yorker*, titled "Feature Presentation," discusses the decline in popularity of objects encumbered by too many features, a phenomenon called "feature creep."

5 According to its website, "The Long Now Foundation was established in 01996* to...become the seed of a very long-term cultural institution. The Long Now Foundation hopes to provide counterpoint to today's accelerating culture and help make long-term thinking more common. We hope to creatively foster responsibility in the framework of the next 10,000 years.... *The Long Now Foundation uses five-digit dates; the extra zero is to solve the deca-millennium bug which will come into effect in about 8,000 years."

6 When going to Dubai, make sure you bring not only your bathing suit but also your favorite ski goggles, because chances are you will visit the Snow Dome for a quick downhill race on the perfect powdery slope in order to escape the 110-degree temperature outside; and when ordering at a McDonald's drive-thru, don't be fooled into thinking that your interlocutor is in the booth—she might be in Mumbai. The outsourcing of call centers and customer service centers has greatly contributed to the establishment of our new time-space proportion.

7 In the May 28, 2007, issue of the *New Yorker*, an article by Alec Wilkinson titled "Remember This? A Project to Record Everything We Do in Life" reported that the great computer scientist Gordon Bell had in 1998 set out to digitize and archive his whole life, from childhood pictures and health records to coffee mugs. The project is still in process.

labor to give objects souls and personality and to ease their communication with people and with other objects.[4] They apply the same bottom-up methodology to spawn innovations that are organically attuned to human nature and to the world, and they rework priorities so that human beings always come before any celebration of progress, as in the project One Laptop per Child or in Jonathan Harris's moving Internet interface We Feel Fine. These designers domesticate innovation and make sure that objects will deliver value and meaning and therefore justify their presence in people's lives, as with Mathieu Lehanneur's delicately high-tech Elements. And out of consideration for people's well-being, they help us incorporate healthy behaviors within our frenetic habits, as seen in Marie-Virginie Berbet's Narco office capsule.

The idea of human scale has changed since Charles and Ray Eames's famous 1968 film Powers of Ten because human perception has been expanded and augmented by technology. Distance is not what it used to be, and neither is time: not only does it range from the attosecond ($10^{-18}$ seconds, or the time it takes for light to travel the length of three hydrogen atoms) to the Long Now, the concept that inspired Danny Hillis to establish a foundation whose goal is to promote thinking for the next ten thousand years, but some professionals' routine commute is a twice-a-month Tokyo–New York round trip, while others work across several time zones without a need to state their position at any time.[5] Indeed, where and when have become hard to pin down on any who.[6] There is a standoff between the two ancient Greek notions of time: chronos, the shared convention of sequential time marked by the sundial, and kairos, the subjective moment that allows an individual to adapt and evolve with circumstances. While no one would argue that we are beholden to the former, the shift toward the latter is seen in the urge to record and share personal, life-defining moments that is at the source of the proliferation of Weblogs and other tagged and mapped metadiaries. This obsessive chronicling of personal information online—from pets' names to breakfast preferences, the phenomenon of oversharing is frequent and is the subject of several etiquette-themed discussions—points to people's attempts to share their epiphanies and impose their own individual experiences of time, memory, and life over the global network that runs on conventional time. Counting on extraordinary advances in data storage capacity and on new, easy-to-use software, we can finally sit back and remember everything.[7] From the revelation that women do not need to have menstrual periods to studies whose goal is to dramatically reduce the amount of sleep needed in order to be perfectly functional and even the debate on human lifespan—which some say soon could be stretched at least half again as

8 Amazing things are happening in the realm of the senses. Scientists and technologists are focusing on hearing, for instance, and on its untapped potential. Several researchers are experimenting on sonocytology, a way to diagnose cancer by listening to cells—or better, by reading sonograms. Professor James K. Gimzewski and Andrew E. Pelling at the UCLA Department of Chemistry first made the discovery that yeast cells oscillate at the nanoscale in 2002. Amplifying this oscillation results in a sound that lies within the human audible range. As far as olfaction is concerned, one study has explored how certain dogs can sniff cancer in a person's breath (Michael McCulloch, Tadeusz Jezierski, Michael Broffman, Alan Hubbard, Kirk Turner, and Teresa Janecki, "Diagnostic Accuracy of Canine Scent Detection in Early- and Late-Stage Lung and Breast Cancers," *Integrative Cancer Therapies* 3 [March 2006]: 30-39).

9 The champion of this attitude is renowned design critic Don Norman, whose work is directly aimed at product designers.

10 Anthony Dunne, interview in *Domus* 889 (February 2006): 55. Moreover, the webpage introducing the college's Design Interactions Department reads: "Designers often refer to people as 'users,' or sometimes as 'consumers.' In Design Interactions, we prefer to think of both users and designers as, first and foremost, people. That is, we see ourselves as complex individuals moving through an equally complex, technologically mediated, consumer landscape. Interaction may be our medium in this department, but people are our primary subject, and people cannot be neatly defined and labeled. We are contradictory, volatile, and always surprising. To remember this is to engage fully with the complexities and challenges of both people and the field of interaction design."

long as current expectations—the focus now is on ways to break the temporal rhythms imposed by society in order to customize and personalize them.

If design is to help enable us to live to the fullest while taking advantage of all the possibilities provided by contemporary technology, designers need to make both people and objects perfectly elastic. It will entail some imaginative thinking—not simply following a straight line from A to C passing through B. Several design principles can be used to accomplish this. One recurrent theme in design today is a stronger involvement of the senses to both enhance and integrate the delivery of high-tech functions, as in James Auger and Jimmy Loizeau's and Susana Soares's scent-based projects or in the synesthesia-inspired work of Eyal Burstein and Michele Gauler—both of which demonstrate technology's ability to deepen our sensorial awareness and spectrum.[8]…

Design schools like the Academy of Art and Design in Eindhoven, The Netherlands (offering, for instance, postgraduate courses in Humanitarian Design and Sustainable Style and Interior, Industrial, and Identity Design), or the Royal College of Art, London, focus their courses on senses and sensuality, identity, memory, and on other staples of human life that are as old as humankind—birth, death, love, safety, and curiosity—yet are rendered urgent by the speed with which technology is moving. These principles differ from the so-called human-centered design that functionalist industrial designers of the past fifty years have employed to shift their attention from the object to the "user"; they are reminders of the great responsibility that comes with design's new great power of giving form and meaning to the degrees of freedom opened by the progress of technology.[9] Such a holistic approach calls for the development of well-honed analytical and critical muscles and for a new, self-assured theory of design. At the Royal College of Art, for instance, Anthony Dunne, head of the Design Interactions Department, preaches the importance of "critical design," which he defines as "a way of using design as a medium to challenge narrow assumptions, preconceptions, and givens about the role products play in everyday life."[10] "Design for debate," as this new type of practice is also called, does not always immediately lead to "useful" objects but rather to servings of exotic food for thought whose usefulness is revealed by their capacity to help us ponder how we really want our things to fit into our lives. Noam Toran's Accessories for Lonely Men and IDEO's Social Mobiles comment on, respectively, solitude and the need for a new etiquette in the age of wireless communication. And we certainly need such meditation more than we need another mobile phone design.

Indeed, even as technology offers us more and more options, many agree that we in fact require fewer—not more—objects in our lives. This very simple belief unites the diverse and yet similarly idealistic efforts of many designers worldwide who are trying to inform our lives with the same economy of energy and materials as found in nature. In addition to balancing our lives with the imperatives of new technology, designers today must also consider the impact of their creations on the environment. Organic design has had many different connotations in history, but in its most contemporary meaning it encompasses not only the enthusiastic exploration of natural forms and structures but also interpretations of nature's economical frameworks and systems. It emerges from the rapidly growing realization that we need to learn to use less matter and energy and to be more efficient. Several factors make contemporary organic design radically different from its past expressions. Towering among these is the computer, whose capacity to master complexity has, perhaps surprisingly, allowed a closeness to the forms and structures of nature never achieved before. Moreover, the urgent need to manage nature's resources more thoughtfully and economically has provoked a sense of responsibility that is felt—or at least worn as a badge—by contemporary thinkers and doers. This trend can be seen in the pervasive use of the term DNA and the suffix "-scape" to describe any kind of organically integrated context (e.g., "home-scape") and of biologically inspired attributes, such as "cellular," to describe the organic skeleton of such entities as the organization of new religious sects, lighting systems, and buildings. Even "viral" has taken on a positive meaning by indicating successful infectious and self-replicating design and communication phenomena.

When it comes to design, however, a badge is not enough: According to an annual review by Britain's Design Council, 80 percent of the environmental impact of the products, services, and infrastructures around us is determined at the design stage.[11] Design needs to engage directly and develop further some of the tools it is currently experimenting with, such as biomimicry algorithms and other forms of computational design, and nanotechnology.[12] Nanotechnology, in particular, offers the promise of the principle of self-assembly and self-organization that one can find in cells, molecules, and galaxies; the idea that you would need only to give the components of an object a little push for the object to come together and reorganize in different configurations could have profound implications for the environment, including energy and

11 Design Council, *Annual Review 2002* (London: 2002): 19.

12 As the Biomimicry.net website reads, "Biomimicry (from *bios*, meaning life, and *mimesis*, meaning to imitate) is a design discipline that studies nature's best ideas and then imitates these designs and processes to solve human problems." The Biomimicry Institute and its president, Janine M. Benyus, author of the 1997 book *Biomimicry* (New York: William Morrow), which popularized this field of study, is a resource for designers and companies interested in learning to observe nature and apply the same type of economical wisdom to issues ranging from mundane to existential, such as how to reduce our erosion of the world's resources.

material savings. "In nanotechnology, new materials and structures can be built atom by atom or molecule by molecule," explains the introduction to the course "Nano and Design" taught by engineer extraordinaire Cecil Balmond at the University of Pennsylvania, while algorithms are described by architects Chris Lasch and Benjamin Aranda as "a macro, a series of steps, a recipe for making bread." In the blog that complements his book *Soft Machines*, Richard Jones extols the potential of nanotechnology in several areas, among them medicine, and talks about "persuading…cells to differentiate, to take up the specialized form of a particular organ," listing several reasons why nanotechnology would be beneficial to a sustainable energy economy.[13]

All these tools are about giving objects basic yet precise instructions and letting them fully develop and connect in networks and systems, and this is where one of the most powerful new directions for design lies. While traditional design is often about cutting existing materials to shape or, in the best cases, taming and adapting them, computational design and nanodesign are about generating objects, as can be seen in embryonic and conceptual examples such as Christopher Woebken's *New Sensual Interfaces*, and also about seeing them adapt to different circumstances, as in Chuck Hoberman's *Emergent Surface* responsive architecture.

As they advocate and obtain roles that are more and more integral to the evolution of society, designers find themselves at the center of an extraordinary wave of cross-pollination. Design-centered interdisciplinary conferences have existed for decades, traditionally initiated by designers.[14] Only recently have other communities started to seek designers' contributions, but this is only the beginning. To adapt and master new technologies and directions, design has branched out into dozens of specialized applications, from communication to interaction and from product design to biomimicry. On the other hand, in order to be truly effective, designers should dabble in economics, anthropology, bioengineering, religion, and cognitive sciences, to mention just a few of the subjects they need today in order to be well-rounded agents of change. Because of their role as intermediaries between research and production, they often act as the main interpreters in interdisciplinary teams, called upon not only to conceive objects, but also to devise scenarios and strategies. To cope with this responsibility, designers should set the foundations for a strong theory of design—something that is today still missing—and become astute generalists. At that point, they will be in a unique position to become the repositories of contemporary culture's need for analysis and synthesis, society's new pragmatic intellectuals.

13  Engineer Cecil Balmond (of Arup), assisted by Jenny Sabin, teaches in the University of Pennsylvania's School of Design, in the Department of Architecture. The quotation was taken from a description of the course for the spring 2007 semester. It continues, "The *nano* prefix means one-billionth, so a nanometer is one-billionth of a meter. Just as antibiotics, the silicon transistor, and plastics…nanotechnology is expected to have profound influences in the twenty-first century, ranging from nanoscopic machines that could for instance be injected in the body to fix problems and the creation of artificial organs and prosthetics, all the way to self-assembling electronic components that behave like organic structures and better materials that perform in novel ways." Chris Lasch and Benjamin Aranda, in a conversation with the author on March 14, 2007, talked about the role of algorithms in architecture, also well explained in their incisive volume *Tooling* (New York: Princeton Architectural Press, 2005). Richard A. L. Jones's blog (www.softmachines.org) is a precious resource for all those who want more information on the potential practical applications of nanotechnology in our future.

14  A few of my personal favorites: the historical International Design Conference in Aspen, now defunct, the ongoing TED (Technology, Entertainment, Design, founded by Richard Saul Wurman and now run by Chris Anderson), and Doors of Perception (founded and still run by John Thackara).

IN 1987, WHILE WORKING AT APPLE, HUGH DUBBERLY COWROTE *KNOWLEDGE NAVIGATOR,*
A VISIONARY FILM THAT PREDICTED NOT ONLY THE FUTURE OF TABLET COMPUTING, BUT THE
CENTRALITY OF THE INTERNET IN THE WORK LIFE OF INDIVIDUALS.[1] Dubberly's practice at the time
focused on traditional corporate communications and branding. But, as *Knowledge Navigator* demonstrated,
he understood even then that future designers would have to negotiate complex networked environments,
systems within systems—ecosystems. Dubberly went on to engage deeply with interactive design, first at Apple,
then at Netscape, and ultimately through his own consultancy, Dubberly Design Office. As he asserts below,
design values and approaches that grew out of the manufacturing world are shifting over. Design, and design
education, should look to an organic-systems model as as we enter the age of biology.

1 Alan Kay contributed to the concept of *Knowledge Navigator.* John Sculley premiered the film as part of his keynote at Educom, a higher-education conference. To read more about this, see Bud Colligan, "How the Knowledge Navigator Video Came About," *Dubberly Design Office,* November 20, 2011, http://www.dubberly.com/articles/how-the-knowledge-navigator-video-came-about.html.

# DESIGN IN THE AGE OF BIOLOGY:
## SHIFTING FROM A MECHANICAL-OBJECT ETHOS TO AN ORGANIC-SYSTEMS ETHOS

### HUGH DUBBERLY | 2008

In the early twentieth century, our understanding of physics changed rapidly; now our understanding of biology is undergoing a similar rapid shift.

Freeman Dyson wrote: "It is likely that biotechnology will dominate our lives and our economic activities during the second half of the twenty-first century, just as computer technology dominated our lives and our economy during the second half of the twentieth."[2]

2 Freeman Dyson, "The Question of Global Warming," *New Yorker* 55, no. 10 (June 2008).

Recent breakthroughs in biology are largely about information—understanding how organisms encode it, store, reproduce, transmit, and express it—mapping genomes, editing DNA sequences, mapping cell-signaling pathways. Changes in our understanding of physics, accompanied by rapid industrialization, led to profound cultural shifts: changes in our view of the world and our place in it. In this context, modernism arose. Similarly, recent changes in our understanding of biology are beginning to create new industries and may bring another round of profound cultural shifts: new changes in our view of the world and our place in it. Already we can see the process beginning. Where once we described computers as mechanical minds, increasingly we describe computer networks with more biological terms—bugs, viruses, attacks, communities, social capital, trust, identity.

## HOW IS DESIGN CHANGING?

Over the past thirty years, the growing presence of electronic information technology has changed the context and practice of design. Changes in the production tools that designers use (software tools, computers, networks, digital displays, and printers) have altered the pace of production and the nature of specifications. But production tools have not significantly changed the way designers think about practice. In a sense, graphic designer Paul Rand was correct when he said, "The computer is just another tool, like the pencil," suggesting the computer would not change the fundamental nature of design.[3]

But computer-as-production-tool is only half the story; the other half is computer-plus-network-as-media.

Changes in the media that designers use (the Internet and related services) have altered what designers make and how their work is distributed and consumed. New media are changing the way designers think about practice and creating new types of jobs. For many of us, both what we design and how we design are substantially different from a generation ago.

## WHAT DO ELECTRONIC MEDIA AND DESIGNING HAVE TO DO WITH BIOLOGY?

Emerging design practice is largely information based, awash in the technologies of information processing and networking. Increasingly, design shares with biology a focus on information flow, on networks of actors operating at many levels, and exchanging the information needed to balance communities of systems. Modern design practice arose alongside the industrial revolution. Design has long been tied to manufacturing—to the reproduction of objects in editions or "runs." The cost of planning and preparation (the cost of design) was small compared with the cost of tooling, materials, manufacturing, and distribution. A mistake in design multiplied thousands of times in manufacturing is difficult and expensive to fix.

The realities of manufacturing led to certain practices and in turn to a set of values or even a way of thinking. In the "modern" era, design practice adopted something of the point of view or philosophy of manufacturing—a mechanical object ethos.

Now as software and services have become a large part of the economy, manufacturing no longer dominates. The realities of producing software and services are very different from those of manufacturing products.

The cost of software (and "content") is almost entirely in planning, preparation, and coding (the cost of design). The cost of tooling, materials, manufacturing, and distribution is small in comparison. Delaying a piece

3 Paul Rand, personal conversation with author during a visit to the Art Center College of Design, Pasadena, Calif., 1993.

of software to "perfect" it invites disaster. Customers have come to expect updates and accept their role as an extension of developers' QA teams, finding "bugs" that can be fixed in the next "patch."

Services also have a different nature from hardware products. "Services are activities or events that create an experience through an interaction—a performance co-created at point-of-delivery."[4] Services are largely intangible, as much about process as final product. They are about a series of experiences across a range of related touch points.

4 Shelley Evenson, "Designing for Service: A Hands-On Introduction," presentation at CMU's Emergence Conference, Pittsburgh, Pa., September 2006.

Just as manufacturing formed its own ethos, software and service development is also forming its own ethos. The realities of software and service development lead to certain practices and to a set of values or even a way of thinking. Emerging design practice is adopting something of the point of view or philosophy of software and service development—an organic-systems ethos.

## MODELS OF CHANGE

Several critics have commented on facets of the change from mechanical-object ethos to organic-systems ethos. This article brings together a series of models outlining the change and contrasting each ethos.

The models are presented in the form of an "era analysis." Two or more eras (e.g., existing emerging eras or specified time periods) are presented as columns in a matrix with rows representing qualities or dimensions, which change across each era and characterize it.

The eras are framed as stark dichotomies to characterize the nature of changes. But experience is typically more fluid, resting along a continuum somewhere between extremes.

| THE END OF INCREMENTALISM | |
| --- | --- |
| *From (escape the past)* | *To (invent the future)* |
| Mechanistic worldview | Ecological-evolutionary worldview |
| Landscape depletion | Landscape renewal |
| Surface novelty | Evocative structures |
| Detached expert | Collaboration |
| Tangible assets | Intangible assets |
| Consolidation | Flow |

*Adapted from John Rheinfrank*

John Rheinfrank provided a broad summary of the change, which may serve as an introduction and an overview.[5] He described a change in worldview similar to the change in ethos described above.

5 John Rheinfrank, "The Philosophy of (User) Experience," presentation at CHI 2002/AIGA Experience Design Forum, Minneapolis, Minn., May 2002.

We may expand Rheinfrank's model to describe how things come to be and the role of designers and their clients in the process....

| PRINCIPLES OF ORGANIZATION | | |
|---|---|---|
| | *Mechanical-object* | *Organic-system* |
| *Economic era* | Industrial Age | Information Age |
| *Paradigm author* | Newton | Darwin |
| *Metaphor* | Clockworks | Ecologies |
| *Values* | Seek simplicity | Embrace complexity |
| *Control* | Top down | Bottom up |
| *Development* | From outside<br>Externally assembled<br>Made | From inside<br>Self-organizing<br>Grown |
| *Designer as* | Author | Facilitator |
| *Designer's role* | Deciding | Building agreement |
| *Client as* | Owner | Steward |
| *Relationship* | Request for approval | Conversation |
| *Stopping condition* | Almost perfect | Good enough for now |
| *Result* | More deterministic | Less predictable |
| *End state* | Completed | Adapting or evolving |
| *Tempo* | Editions | Continuous updating |

*Adapted from Hugh Dubberly and Paul Pangaro[6]*

6  Hugh Dubberly and Paul Pangaro, joint course development, Stanford, 2000-2008.

## A CONCERN FOR USERS

As Rheinfrank pointed out, the designer is moving from detached expert to collaborator. And the relationship between designer and constituent is moving from expert-patient to what Horst Rittel called "a symmetry of ignorance (or expertise)," where the views of all constituents are equally valid in defining project goals.[7] Liz Sanders presents a similar argument with slightly different eras, introducing moving beyond human-centered or user-centered design.[8]

7  Horst Rittel, "On the Planning Crisis: Systems Analysis of 'First and Second Generations.'" *Bedrifts Økonomen* 8 (1972): 390-396.

8  Liz Sanders, "Generative Design Thinking" presentation, San Francisco, June 2007.

| RELATIONSHIP BETWEEN DESIGNER AND AUDIENCE | | | |
|---|---|---|---|
| | *Past* | *Current* | *Emerging* |
| Design Paradigm | Expert driven | Human centered | Facilitated |
| Audience Role | Customer | User | Participant |
| Activity | Consume | Experience | Co-create |
| | • shop | • use | • adapt/modify/extend |
| | • buy | • interact | • design |
| | • own | • communicate | • make |

*Adapted from Liz Sanders*

Co-development is also a fundamental tenet of open-source software. Eric Raymond wrote, "Treating your users as co-developers is your least-hassle route to rapid code improvement and debugging." He added, "Even at a higher level of design, it can be very valuable to have lots of co-developers random walking through the design space near your product." Raymond famously contrasted "cathedrals carefully crafted by individual wizards or small bands of magi working in splendid isolation" to "a great babbling bazaar of differing agendas and approaches." He suggested traditional "a priori" approaches will be bested by "self-correcting systems of selfish agents."[9]

9 Eric Raymond, "The Cathedral and the Bazaar," v3.0, 2000, available at http://www.catb.org/~esr/writings/cathedral-bazaar/cathedral-bazaar/cathedral-bazaar.ps.

| THE CATHEDRAL | VS. | THE BAZAAR |
|---|---|---|
| Commercial | | Free licenses |
| Proprietary | | Open source |
| Fewer paid workers | | More volunteers |
| Heavily managed | | Loosely coupled |
| Hierarchical | | Distributed peer review |
| Serial processes | | Massively parallel debugging |
| Longer development cycles | | More frequent releases |

*Adapted from Eric Raymond*

## THE RISE OF SERVICE DESIGN

The shift from industrial age to information age mirrors, in part, a shift from manufacturing economy to service economy. In the new economy, as former *Wired* editor Kevin Kelly put it, "Commercial products are best treated as though they were services. It's not what you sell a customer, it's what you do for them. It's not what something is, it's what it is connected to, what it does. Flows become more important than resources. Behavior counts."[10]

10 Kevin Kelly, *Out of Control: The New Biology of Machines, Social Systems, and the Economic World* (New York: Addison Wesley, 1994).

Early on, Shelley Evenson saw the importance of service design, and she has led U.S. designers in developing the field. She has provided a framework contrasting traditional business-planning methods with service-design methods. Her framework parallels the larger change in ethos we've been discussing.

| A SHIFT IN DEVELOPMENT MODELS | Product | Service |
|---|---|---|
| *Era* | Planned | Emergent |
| *Focus* | Find the right strategy | Understand customers |
| *Growth* | Top down | Organic |
| *Method* | Sequential | Parallel |
| *Delivery* | Internal | Co-produced |

*Adapted from Shelley Evenson*[11]

11 Shelley Evenson, "Experience Strategy: Product/Service Systems," presentation, Detroit, 2006.

Typically, responsibility for designing individual artifacts rests pretty much with one individual, but systems design almost by definition requires teams of people (often including many specialties of design). The need for teams of designers can be seen easily in the design of software systems and service systems, where many artifacts, touch points, and subsystems must be coordinated in a community of cooperating systems. For example,

HUGH DUBBERLY
Interview with
Steven Heller
2006

"Web-based services" or "integrated systems of hardware, software, and networked applications" require development and management teams with many specialties.

The work of an individual designer on an individual artifact has often been characterized as "hand-craft." In contrast, Paul Pangaro and I have proposed "service-craft" to describe "the design, management, and ongoing development of service systems." Design practice in a hand-craft context differs markedly from design practice in a service-craft context. Having assembled a team, care must be taken to negotiate goals, set expectations, define processes, and communicate project status and changes in direction. Care must also be taken to create opportunities for new language to emerge and to create capacity for coevolution between service and participants.

| CHANGES IN DESIGN PRACTICE | | |
|---|---|---|
| | Hand-craft | Service-craft |
| Subject | Things | Behaviors |
| Participant(s) | Individual | Team |
| Thinking | Intuitive | Reasoned |
| Language | Idiosyncratic | Shared |
| Process | Implicit | Explicit |
| Nature of work | Concrete | Abstracted |
| Key skill | Drawing | Modeling |
| Construction | Direct | Mediated |

Adapted from Hugh Dubberly and Paul Pangaro

We also noted that "hand-craft has not gone away, nor is service-craft divorced from hand-craft. Hand-craft plays a role in service-craft (just as in developing software applications, coding remains a form of hand-craft). While service-craft focuses on behavior, it supports behavior with artifacts. While service-craft requires teams, teams rely on individuals. Service-craft does not replace hand-craft; rather, service-craft extends or builds another layer upon hand-craft."[12]…

12 Hugh Dubberly and Paul Pangaro, "Cybernetics and Service-Craft: Language for Behavior-Focused Design," *Kybernetes* 36, no. 9/10 (April 2007).

## SUSTAINABLE DESIGN

The mechanical-object/organic-system dichotomy also appears vividly in discussions about ecology. Much of our economy still depends on "consumers" buying products, which we eventually throw "away." William McDonough and Michael Braungart have pointed out that there is no "away," that in nature, "waste is food." They urged us to think in terms of "cradle to cradle" cycles of materials use, and they suggested manufacturers

13  William McDonough and Michael Braungart, *Cradle to Cradle: Remaking the Way We Make Things* (New York: North Point Press, 2002).

lease products and reclaim them for reuse.[13] Theirs is another important perspective on the idea of product as service.

Architects, too, have begun to design for disassembly and reconfiguration. Herman Miller recently published a manifesto on programmable environments, talking about the need for "pliancy" in the built environment and echoing the language of *The Cathedral and the Bazaar* while discussing building design.[14]

14  Jim Long, Jennifer Magnolfi, and Lois Maasen, *Always Building: The Programmable Environment* (Zeeland, Mich.: Herman Miller Creative Office, 2008).

Sustainable design is emerging as an issue of intense concern for designers, manufacturers, and the public. The same sort of systems thinking required for software and service design is also required for sustainable design. This provides further impetus for changing our approach to design education.

Stuart Walker, professor of design at the University of Calgary, has written, "Only by fundamentally changing our approaches to deal with the new circumstances can we hope to develop new models for design and production that are more compatible with sustainable ways of living. Wrestling with existing models and trying to modify them is not an effective strategy."

| REFRAMING DESIGN | |
| --- | --- |
| *Conventional design* | *Sustainable design* |
| Industrial design | Design of functional objects |
| Product design | Creation of material culture |
| Specialization | Improvisation |
| Conventional | Uncertain, uncomfortable |
| Professional | Amateur, dilettante (acting with love and joy) |
| Specific | Holistic, integrative |
| Instrumental | Intrinsic |
| Problem solving | Experimenting |
| Solutions | Possibilities |
| A priori design | Contingent design |

*Adapted from Stuart Walker[15]*

15  Stuart Walker, *Sustainable by Design: Explorations in Theory and Practice* (London: Earthscan, 2006).

## EARLY PARALLELS

The current shift from a mechanical-object ethos to an organic-systems ethos has been anticipated in earlier shifts.

In the mid-1960s, architects and designers began to focus on "rational" design methods, borrowing from the successes of large military-engineering projects during the war and the years following it. While these methods were effective for military projects with clear objectives, they often proved unsuccessful in the face of social problems with complex and competing objectives. For example, methods suited to building missiles were applied to large-scale construction in urban-redevelopment projects, but those methods proved unsuited to addressing the underlying social problems that redevelopment projects sought to cure.

Horst Rittel proposed a second generation of design methods, effectively reframing the movement, casting design as conversation about "wicked problems."[16] His proposal came too late or too early for the design world, which had already moved on to "postmodernism" but had not yet encountered the Internet.

Rittel's work did attract attention in computer science (he was a pioneer in using computers in design planning), where "design rationale" (the process of tracking issues and arguments related to a project) continues as a field of research. More recently, Rittel's work has attracted attention in business school publications addressing innovation and design management.[17, 18]

16 Ibid.

17 Jeanne Liedtka, "Strategy as Design," *Rotman Management* (Winter 2004): 12–15.

18 John C. Camillus, "Strategy as a Wicked Problem," *Harvard Business Review* (May 2008): 99–106.

| **1960s MECHANISTIC APPROACHES PROVOKED 1970s REACTION** | | |
|---|---|---|
| | *First-gen design methods* | *Second-gen design methods* |
| **Approach** | Design as optimization | Design as argument |
| | Problem solving | Goal framing |
| | Linear or waterfall | Multilevel feedback |
| **Domain** | Science | Design |
| | Design as part of science | Design as its own domain |
| | Sciences of the artificial | Designing for evolution |
| **Stance** | Neutral, objective | Political, subjective |
| **Mode** | Descriptive "What is…" | Speculative "What could be…" |
| **Time horizon** | Present | Future |
| **Knowledge** | Factual | Instrumental |

*Adapted from Horst Rittel by Chanpory Rith[19]*

19 Chanpory Rith, personal communication with author, 2 July 2005.

Paul Pangaro and I have also noted that Rittel's framing of first- and second-generation design methods parallels Heinz von Foerster's framing of first- and second-order cybernetics. Von Foerster described a shift of focus in cybernetics from mechanism to language and from systems observed (from the outside) to systems that observe (observing systems).

| **CYBERNETICS MATURES** | | |
|---|---|---|
| | *First-order cybernetics* | *Second-order cybernetics* |
| | Single loop | Double loop |
| | Control loops | Learning loops |
| | Regulating in environment | Participating in conversation |
| | Observed systems | Observing systems |
| | Observer outside frame | Observer in frame |
| | Observer describes goal | Participants co-create goals |
| | Assumes objectivity | Recognizes subjectivity |

*Adapted from Paul Pangaro[20]*

20 Paul Pangaro, personal communications with author, 2000–2008.

In 1958 von Foerster formed the Biological Computer Laboratory at the University of Illinois Urbana-Champaign. He brought in Ross Ashby as a professor and later Gordon Pask and Humberto Maturana as visiting research professors. The lab focused on problems of self-organizing systems and provided an alternative to the more mechanistic approach of AI [artificial intelligence] followed at MIT by Marvin Minsky and others.[21] In a way, von Foerster anticipated the shift from mechanical-object ethos to organic-systems ethos in computing, design, and perhaps the larger culture.

21  Albert Müller, "A Brief History of the BCL: Heinz von Foerster and the Biological Computer Laboratory," *Österreichische Zeitschrift für Geschichtswissenschaften* 11, no. 1 (2000): 9–30. Translated by Jeb Bishop and since republished in "An Unfinished Revolution?"

## WHAT DO THESE CHANGES MEAN FOR DESIGN EDUCATION?

As design moves into the age of biology and shifts from a mechanical-object ethos to an organic-systems ethos, we should reflect on how best to prepare for coming changes in practice. At a recent conference on design education, Meredith Davis described "the distance between where we are going in the practice of graphic design and longstanding assumptions about design education."[22]…

22  Meredith Davis, "Toto, I've Got a Feeling We're Not in Kansas Anymore…," presentation at the AIGA Design Education Conference, Boston, April 2008.

Davis (building on [Sharon] Poggenpohl and [Jürgen] Habermas) distinguished between two models of practice, "know how" and "know that," "design as a craft and design as a discipline." This distinction parallels the distinction between hand-craft and service-craft that Pangaro and I propose above. Davis asserted, "college design curricula, and the pedagogies through which we deliver them, are based almost exclusively on the first model of practice, on know how, and don't acknowledge issues that drive emerging practices."

Davis's argument and framing are closely related to changes described in this article. Changes that Davis advocates are consistent with the spirit of the new ethos and aimed at helping designers grasp the nature of organic-systems work and preparing them for practice in the age of biology.

Of course, not all designers welcome the coming change. Form giving remains a large part of design practice and design education. Will some designers be able to continue to practice primarily as form givers? That seems likely. But already a schism is developing both in design practice and design education, as individuals and institutions choose to focus on either form giving or on planning. It remains to be seen if one person, one firm, or one school can bridge the divide and excel at both.

IN 2008 AMSTERDAM-BASED DESIGNERS LUNA MAURER, EDO PAULUS, JONATHAN PUCKEY, AND ROEL WOUTERS BEGAN GATHERING ON TUESDAY NIGHTS AROUND MAURER'S KITCHEN TABLE. Since they found it difficult to define their combined practices with a term limited to a specific medium, such as graphic design or interaction design, they decided instead to articulate a way of thinking. After months of weekly discussions, they developed the Conditional Design Manifesto. The resulting principles guided them through a wide range of individual and collaborative exercises and projects that privileged process: input, output, logic, and subjectivity. Using both digital and physical materials the Conditional Design members established strict parameters and then put systems into play. Their approach harkens back to Karl Gerstner's experiments with design as a range of possible permutations and to artist Sol LeWitt's instructions for wall drawings.[1] Unlike these 1960s methodologies, however, Maurer, Paulus, Puckey, and Wouters ultimately strive to create systems that take on lives of their own. As Maurer notes, "From simple rules and ingredients, complex things can happen. Behaviors emerge....The system talks back to you."[2] As the group's members maintain in their manifesto, they want "to reflect the here and now." Their practice moves beyond the unified formal and conceptual systems of modernism to take on the complex structures and behaviors made possible by the exponential growth of computing.[3]

1  To read more about connections with Sol LeWitt and Karl Gerstner, see Andrew Blauvelt, "Ghost in the Machine: Distributing Subjectivity," in *Conditional Design Workbook* (Amsterdam: Valiz, 2003), iii-vi.

2  Interview with the author, October 7, 2010.

3  In addition to the Conditional Design collective, Maurer, Wouters, and Puckey formed a new design studio, Moniker, in 2012.

# CONDITIONAL DESIGN:
## A MANIFESTO FOR ARTISTS AND DESIGNERS

**LUNA MAURER, EDO PAULUS, JONATHAN PUCKEY, ROEL WOUTERS | 2008**

Through the influence of the media and technology on our world, our lives are increasingly characterized by speed and constant change. We live in a dynamic, data-driven society that is continually sparking new forms of human interaction and social contexts. Instead of romanticizing the past, we want to adapt our way of working to coincide with these developments, and we want our work to reflect the here and now. We want to embrace the complexity of this landscape, deliver insight into it, and show both its beauty and its shortcomings.

Our work focuses on processes rather than products: things that adapt to their environment, emphasize change, and show difference.

Instead of operating under the terms of Graphic Design, Interaction Design, Media Art, or Sound Design, we want to introduce Conditional Design as a term that refers to our approach rather than our chosen media. We conduct our activities using the methods of philosophers, engineers, inventors, and mystics.

**LUNA MAURER**
Interview with
Helen Armstrong
2010

## PROCESS

The process is the product.

The most important aspects of a process are time, relationship, and change.

The process produces formations rather than forms.

We search for unexpected but correlative, emergent patterns.

Even though a process has the appearance of objectivity, we realize the fact that it stems from subjective intentions.

## LOGIC

Logic is our tool.

Logic is our method for accentuating the ungraspable.

A clear and logical setting emphasizes that which does not seem to fit within it.

We use logic to design the conditions through which the process can take place.

Design conditions using intelligible rules.

Avoid arbitrary randomness.

Difference should have a reason.

Use rules as constraints.

Constraints sharpen the perspective on the process and stimulate play within the limitations.

## INPUT

The input is our material.

Input engages logic and activates and influences the process.

Input should come from our external and complex environment: nature, society, and its human interactions.

**BRENDA LAUREL ENGAGES HEAD-ON WITH POP CULTURE. SHE CONSTRUCTS INTERACTIVE ENVIRONMENTS THAT CHALLENGE US TO LOOK BEYOND OUR NEXT CONSUMER FIX SO THAT WE MIGHT ENACT REAL CHANGE IN OUR SOCIETY.** "Design," she advocates, "gives voice to values....A design that has not engaged the designer's values may speak, but with a hollow voice."[1] In 1996 Laurel cofounded the game development firm Purple Moon, whose aim was to produce media that recognized the needs and interests of young girls between eight and fourteen—a market largely ignored by the gaming industry at the time. Although acquired by Mattel in 1999 and shut down, the firm successfully staked out a path for cultivating girls' interest in computation. The insightful research behind Purple Moon, particularly regarding girls' preference for interactive experiences stemming from complex social interactions, fed a broader understanding of gender and gaming.[2] Laurel's current work continues to fuel humanist goals of love and respect through the development of technology informed by empirical research. Her interests now lie in utilizing distributed sensor networks and visualizations of biological data to help decision makers—as well as the rest of us—engage more deeply with the natural world.

1  Brenda Laurel, "Reclaiming Media: Doing Culture Work in These Weird Times," presentation, AIGA National Design Conference, Washington, DC, March 23, 2002), http://voiceconference.aiga.org/transcripts/index.html.

2  To hear more about Laurel's experiences at Purple Moon, watch "Brenda Laurel: Games for Girls," TED, February 1998, http://www.ted.com/talks/brenda_laurel_on_making_games_for_girls.

# DESIGNED ANIMISM

**BRENDA LAUREL | 2009**

My interest in the relationship between pervasive computing and animism has been brewing for some time—an anthropological bent and an engagement with poetics are old friends. I followed Mark Weiser's work on ubiquitous computing at Xerox PARC and witnessed other early developments in the domain at Interval Research. During my time as chair of the graduate Media Design program at Art Center, I was drawn to thinking about ambient and pervasive computing from new perspectives within the world of art and design. When I also joined Sun Labs in 2005, I got to see the development of the Sunspots up close and personal. Of course, it didn't hurt to be married to one of the principal researchers on the spots team, who continued his work with sensor networks at the NASA Ames Research Center. I'm now heading up a new transdisciplinary grad design program at California College of the Arts, where pervasive computing and sensor networks will play a significant role in many of our studios as well as in collaboration with other institutions. I see pervasive computing as an extremely important phase shift in our capabilities, opening up huge new vistas of possibility for design, discovery, experience, and human agency.

BRENDA LAUREL
"Tools for Knowing,
Judging, and
Taking Action in
the Twenty-First
Century"
2000

What does pervasive computing have to do with animism? Essentially, it can become a tool in manifesting what I call "designed animism." The goal is fundamentally experiential, but the consequences are profound: designed animism forms the basis of a poetics for a new world....

I won't attempt to catalog all of the wonderful examples of emergence in natural, social, and computational systems. I want to simply call your attention to emergence as a design resource that can be tapped by networks of sensor-enabled devices working on local rules to create both beauty and knowledge.

So here's a funny thing. In 2005, Sun Labs sponsored a transdisciplinary studio hosted by the Media Design program at Art Center. Bruce Sterling, who was in residence in our studio that year, co-taught the course, along with Nik Hafermaas and Phil van Allen. The idea was to lob a bunch of Sunspots—networked devices that are capable of producing emergent behavior—at a bunch of design students and let them have it. Jed Berk and Nikhil Mittner, both Media Design students, designed a flock of blimps that they called ALAVs—"autonomous lighter-than-air vehicles." The blimps could be "fed" through an array of fiber-optic tubes. When they were "hungry," they descended, and when they were nourished, they lifted off. When they were close to one another, they flocked and cooed. I have to say, it was totally trippy. When I last spoke with Jed, he was attaching video cameras to them and let them create a kind of ambient video blog. Cool.

Cool. So what?...As I said earlier, with animism I am not so concerned with the attribution of spiritual powers to beings and processes in the natural world as I am concerned with what those attributions induce in us. When we see the world as deeply alive and beautiful, how does it change us? How does it change what we decide and do in the world?

My good friend Sean White has been working on a system called an Electronic Field Guide [EFG]. The vision for the project is to explore new forms of field guides that enhance cognition and memory. The project's explicit purpose is to serve botanists and other scientists in identifying plants and observing or visualizing some of the relationships at work in their ecosystems. The project is a large-scale collaboration between Columbia, the Smithsonian, and the University of Maryland. A prototype system has been deployed on Plummers Island and will soon be mounted again at a science station on Barro Colorado Island in Panama. Sean says: "Biologists of all stripes go down there for research and most of them have their own specialty. We are exploring the possibility of providing the EFG to aid researchers in quick identification of flora relevant to their own ecosystem research. If a botanist is studying a caterpillar, they may not be able to identify the species of plants that it eats. The system will help them create an ecological web of relationships and perhaps even help build a semantic web in the field for further eco-informatic study."

Sean has experimented with multiple cameras and sensors as inputs and with hardened tablets, augmented reality displays, and mobile phones as UI [user interface] devices. He believes that a distributed system without centralized control will eventually be an optimal form. He describes his goals this way: "We do this to support being in the world and part of the world." He reports that when people experience these real-time streams of data in combination, a holistic sense of delight often emerges. In other words, emergence happens inside the person, and this is true even when one brain could not possibly sort the specific information content of each of the streams of information that are available to them. He's had botanists tell him that they have felt the boundaries of their bodies dissolve. But, he cautions, this transcendental awareness is fragile and must be approached with a spirit of lightness.

As Sean's system demonstrates, the process that I described in the context of prescientific representations in art and music has its inverse. In the first case, the creation of a representation that delights the artist reveals a deeper intuition of some of the unseen shapes of nature. In the inverse case, the fusion of inputs from distributed sensors delivered in delightful ways creates the same sort of joyous intuition.

When discussing this phenomenon at the 2006 Ubicomp conference, Bruce Sterling asserted in his usual acerbic way that "there is no magic." Sean's project combines sensor data with machine learning techniques to look at covariance in an n-dimensional space and find the eigenvectors or most meaningful axes in that space. Those reveal interesting patterns that a person can experience in sensory ways. They look at frequency patterns with Fourier transforms and the texture of irises with Gabor jets. With semantic zooming they are able to move in and out of the pattern space. Now that's magic!

In my garden, there are fairies.

One of my fairies watches the lavender. This one has a history of the flowers and knowledge of how sun and shade move over the garden as the day passes. The lavender fairy brings the scent of warm flowers into my room just at the sunniest hour. It also whispers with the bee fairy, who knows that when the lavender is just so, the bees will come. The water fairies taste the soil around my plants and drip when they are too dry. The lizard fairies dance around the top of my desk when they see the lizards scurry from the Oregon grapes to the woodpile.

We see fairies, or make them up, but now we can also *make* them. We have, for the first time, the capacity to create entities that can sense and act autonomously, or with one another, or with living beings. They can learn and evolve. They can reveal new patterns, extend our senses, enhance our agency, and change our minds.

My fairies watch the sun set with me. They dance the changes in light and temperature, in the closing of certain flowers, in the quieting of songbirds and the wakening of owls. And I have this perfectly joyful sense that my body is my home, my garden, my canyon, my trees. If I had more sensors, my body could be the earth. With matching effectors, I become a "Gaian Gardener," responsible for and enacting the health of the living planet.

Scientists and artists know that patterns drawn from nature tickle our nervous systems at a deep, preconscious level. Designed animism is a healing system for our disconnect with our planet. But as our history so vividly shows, we are not likely to come to new awareness through fear, or even through information. We may, however, come to it through delight.

WE KNOW THE RULES OF GOOD DESIGN. BUT IT OFTEN COMES AS A DELIGHTFUL REVELATION TO YOUNG DESIGNERS THAT BRILLIANT DESIGN NOT ONLY PERMITS BUT REQUIRES THE DESIGNER'S PERSONAL VOICE.

BRENDA LAUREL
"Reclaiming Media:
Doing Culture Work
in These Weird Times"
2002

**DESIGNER AND BLOGGER KHOI VINH UNDERSTOOD EARLY ON THE PUBLISHING CAPABILITIES OF THE MAC AND THE INTERNET.** It took a bit longer, however, for him to act upon a larger truth. After years of transferring analog design approaches to a digital format, he began to understand that networked technology transforms—rather than repurposes—communication systems. As design director of NYTimes.com from 2005 to 2010, he looked closely at the underlying Web framework for the paper's digital content, facilitating this transformation for the *Times*. He understood that conversations rather than broadcast messages had become the central communicative trope. Designers, as he insists in the text below, have to respond accordingly by crafting favorable conditions for such dialogues. Inspired by the birth of his daughter, he left the *Times* to seize upon entrepreneurial opportunities that later manifested in apps such as Mixel, Wildcard, and Kidpost.[1] "Anything that can be social will be" became his new mantra.[2] When hardware and social software come together, Vinh observes, the barriers between disciplines such as journalism, photography, video, and art fall away. The result: a more creatively aware, innovative society.

1 To learn more about Vinh's early years as a designer, listen to Debbie Millman, "Design Matters with Debbie Millman: Khoi Vin," podcast audio, April 13, 2012, http://www.debbiemillman.com/designmatters/khoi-vinh/.

2 To read more about using social media to lower the barriers to art, watch the video of his Insights lecture at the Walker Art Center in March 2012, https://www.youtube.com/watch?v=kKOMBA3ps64.

# CONVERSATIONS WITH THE NETWORK

**KHOI VINH | 2011**

The design world that I came up in—the graphic design industry at the end of the last century—was fundamentally about fashioning *messages*: ornamenting and embellishing content so that a core idea, product, or service could be more effectively consumed. Even if a designer felt compelled to obscure the content, as was the style of the postmodern discourse that dominated the field at the time, the operative notion was that design was fundamentally about the transmission of messages.

It took nearly a decade of working in digital media before I understood that this idea was fundamentally at odds with the new archetype inherent in networked technology. To be sure, digital media is conducive to communication; in fact, the Internet is perhaps the greatest multiplier of communication that the world has even seen. With its enormous and pervasive reach it transmits ideas across great distances with great speed, among a large number of people, and in unbelievably rapid succession, all as a matter of course. In many ways such freedom and efficiency have drastically democratized communication, obsolescing the more deliberate, thoughtful pace that communication took when mediated by graphic design. But in this new world designers are critical not so much for the transmission of messages but for the crafting of the spaces within which those messages can be borne.

VERY OFTEN IT SEEMS TO ME THAT REGULAR PEOPLE SEEM
TO UNDERSTAND TECHNOLOGY BETTER THAN BIG COMPANIES DO.

KHOI VINH
*Design Matters*
*with Debbie Millman*
2012

To understand this difference, it's helpful to look back at the predigital world and recognize that the predominant notion of how design worked was this: every design solution was the product of a visionary who birthed and nurtured an original idea, a radical insight, or an inspired revision. The designer gave it life and labored over it, so that the original inspiration evolved into a complete and definitive work. There was no design without the designer.

It was a useful construct through which to comprehend design: the idea that a single person (or group of people) was responsible for a design solution allowed hopeful young designers like me to understand this mystery as something achievable on human terms. It made inspiration knowable and potentially reproducible, provided role models, archetypes to aspire to. If genius could be embodied in a single person, then anyone might be a genius, or at least, with work and discipline, could learn from the ways of their design heroes. These heroes could be interviewed, written about, studied, even encountered in the real world at lectures and conferences. They walked among us; if we were lucky we might even come to know them personally.

In this model the designer was something of a storyteller, and the finished design functioned as a kind of narrative. The designer created the beginning, middle, and end, leading the audiences through something immersive, wondrous, bracing, satisfying, and/or inspiring. Thus the core product, whether an advertisement, magazine, article, or consumer object, would be transformed into a visual story: an ad for a museum might become a map of the human body, an interview with a musician might become a travelogue of an alternative mindscape, a jar of pasta sauce might evoke a classical age lost to contemporary sensibilities. Whatever the conceit, the audience was beholden to the designer's grand plan, experiencing the design according to those original intentions. The closer the audience's experience to the designer's original script, the more effective the designer.

Many of the greatest designers in history have been measured by their ability to tell compelling stories. As an aspirant to the trade, I marveled at Alexey Brodovitch's groundbreaking midcentury work in the pages of *Harper's Bazaar*. Brodovitch forged hypermodern tales of glamour from expertly art-directed photography, type, and graphic elements. In each magazine spread he juxtaposed models in unexpected poses with inventive layout, commanding the narrative as effectively as the magazine's editors and writers; in many ways his was the hand that compelled each issue into a coherent whole.

In my early career I also pored over David Carson's deconstructive work from his signature stints as art director at *Beach Culture* and *Ray Gun*. With blown-out type and nearly unreadable text, Carson practically usurped the narrative in favor of his own creative agenda, privileging the relationship between designer and reader while demoting the relationship between the writer and reader; he abstracted his own reading of the content into an unconventional, heady brand of visual narrative, something that spoke to the unique persuasive power that designers possessed.

These were my heroes: Brodovitch, Cipe Pineles, Paul Rand, Alexander Liberman, M. F. Agha, and other originators of the visual storytelling methods still plumbed by designers today, as well as Carson, Rudy VanderLans, Why Not Associates, Ed Fella, P. Scott Makela, Neville Brody, and the rest of the graphic-design insurgents who were then at the frontiers of design authorship. It's not easy to rationalize such divorced bodies of work into a coherent influence, but what they had in common was that they were all storytellers.

As I pursued a career in interaction design, I saw it as my duty to carry this sensibility over to a new platform. The Internet was then, and today remains, a young medium and I reasoned that it could only benefit from a century's worth of design conventions and lessons accumulated in the world. And in this I made a fundamental miscalculation.

The designer as author, as craftsperson bringing together beginning, middle, and end, becomes redundant in a space in which every participant forges his or her own beginning, middle, and end. And that is exactly what happens in networked media. The narrative recedes, and the behavior of the design solution becomes prominent. What becomes important are questions that concern not the author but the users. How does the system respond to the input of its users? When a user says something to the system, how does the system respond?

Where analog media thrive on the compelling power of narrative, digital media insist on much less linear modes of communication. Instead of the one-to-many model that dominated the last century—for example, a magazine article written by a single journalist and encountered by thousands of readers—the Internet is a many-to-many platform, a framework in which everyone talks to everyone and every utterance might inspire a reply. It is a conversation rather than a broadcast.

Although we are approaching the commercial Internet's third decade, it feels like we are still in an evolutionary phase, still coming to grips with this transition from narrative to conversation. We remain preoccupied by the residual power of brands built upon aging narrative authorities: the major broadcast networks, the major publishers, and the major record labels and film studios. Yet few of those industries have achieved truly comfortable footholds in the new landscape; they continue to grapple with the new digital paradigm— sometimes elegantly, often fitfully, occasionally with tremendous intolerance.

In part this transitional difficulty can be blamed on the superficial resemblance that digital interfaces can share with artifacts of the analog world: pages, headlines, paragraphs, logos, icons, and photographs are just as common in digital products as they are in print products. Graphic communication appears to be a thread common to both analog and digital worlds, so for many like me, who came from the former, it has only been natural to try to apply narrative thinking to the latter. But to understand digital media as a form of narrative is to misread the problem entirely.

Digital media is not a printing press; it does not yield publications but objects of a new kind—some people call them *products*, a decidedly commercial (and not altogether objectionable) term, but I prefer *experiences*. The great experiences of this new medium have no beginning, middle, and end; there is no narrative arc for Google, no measurable breadth for Facebook, no climactic resolution for Twitter. Of course the companies that brought these experiences to life have a narrative of their own: they were founded one day in the not-too-distant past and they will fold one day in the unforeseen future. But in the day-to-day interactions of countless millions of people these experiences exist as a continuum.

Certainly they are coherent environments of pages, headlines, paragraphs, logos, icons, and photos, but they are also an amalgam of invisible user cues, organizational structures, intentional and unintentional system responses, ambient content, constantly regenerating activity, and, most important, reflections of each user, in the content, in the ornamentation, in the very personality of the experience.

To design these systems is to anticipate what cannot be planned, to create a framework in which the unexpected can be expected to happen. The designer's job is not to execute the vision of one person but to establish the conditions under which rich, rewarding conversation can happen. This work occurs at many different levels, from the prompts for user input and the character of system output to the channels for peer dialogue and the continual iteration that takes place over a product's life cycle.

Take the search function. A user enters a term in a search field, and the system reflects back the user's intention and then some; it must respond in a manner that acknowledges the thrust of what was requested, but it must also provide more—more accuracy, more depth, more variety. Just as a conversation between two people must move forward, search results must reiterate what one participant says to the other while simultaneously sharpening and broadening the subject of discussion.

The search function is perhaps the most common interaction performed today, across every subject, under the aegis of many different brands, and in countless contexts. Yet it is quite often thoroughly unsatisfying, mostly because few systems can participate in sufficiently rewarding search-based conversations with their users. I might argue that in spite of its critical importance, searching is so difficult a problem that it has required the most overwhelming combination of human intellect and raw computing power to design a search experience that can adequately converse with users: Google. Its success is well known, but it's still worth emphasizing how thoroughly Google's effectiveness has shaped the Internet experiences designed in the first decade of this century. Designing systems in such a way that their core content is transparent to Google—that is, so that it will be found by Google's remarkably effective search—became a nonnegotiable design principle for countless digital products.

Perhaps because of its inherent difficulty and the fact that few sites have the resources to do it well, searching, in most digital experiences, is designed only as a supplemental feature. In recent years more and more digital experiences have come to rely on the more readily available power between peers; social networks have become so expansively propagated that the conversations between users on these networks threaten to eclipse the primacy of search in terms of directing traffic. Conversations on Facebook and Twitter—status updates, tweets, and other fragmentary bits of communication—can contain within them recommendations, references, asides, and links to other content and Internet destinations that are much richer and more powerful than search results because they originate from trusted sources. As a result we are entering an age in which these conversations can be more effective at driving attention and commerce than results provided by Google and other search engines.

Designing for social media is an exercise in negating the designer's authorial privilege. Experiences that hope to reap the rewards of rich social interactions must be incredibly modest in demonstrating the storytelling skills of the designer, because they are very much in the business of creating the conditions under which these rewarding conversations can happen. They must allow the narrative to recede and the behaviors of the system to come forward.

The most popular social networks—and social networks are always measured in popularity—have been paragons of neutrality. There is a brand presence at Facebook, of course, but it is decidedly less prominent than the artistic showmanship in the pages of any major print magazine. The design of its predecessor, Myspace, was distinguished only as platform for some of the most uninhibited, aesthetically unsound user customization ever brought into the world. And Twitter, that unpredictable outlet for billions of stray thoughts, may be a harbinger of design to come: a design practically without a design. For many users Twitter is experienced through third-party client software; the Twitter logo and the Twitter brand are all but invisible, yet at the same time the experience is indelibly Twitter. This is what digital design looks like when it does away with the biases of the analog world.

But social networks must do more than allow for conversation between users. If they were simply bulletin boards for motivated users on the networks, if their only design challenge was to let those who would talk be heard, they would be something very different. They must also allow for passive conversation, for the thousands of users who pass through a posting without speaking up. These lurkers may mark a post as a favorite or they may make the implicit endorsement of republishing it, or they may forward the post to their own networks; although they take no explicit action, the simple fact of their having viewed a post is automatically recorded. These ghostlike tracks are also a kind of conversation; they say something back to the original poster as well as to themselves—their presence is a participation in itself. Designers who create social experiences must anticipate these marginal but critical behaviors, and there can be a multitude of them—enough so that there is little or no room for the designer to execute expressions of his or her ego. As a design challenge, social media is still new; it is significant in its implications today but will only become more and more so as social networks become more prevalent, more complex, and more diffuse.

In the last decade of the twentieth century it was clear that the Internet would transform everything; now that this has nearly come to pass, it is becoming increasingly evident that social media will do so as well. But part of that transformation is a sense of continual renewal, and this is the last and perhaps the most significant way in which digital media transforms the work of the designer: the designer's challenge is to create a framework for the user to engage in conversation, but the designer is also now charged with engaging the user in conversation through the framework itself. Design solutions can no longer be concluded; they're now works in progress, objects that continually evolve and are continually reinvented. A designer creates a framework for experience, the user conducts experiences within that framework, and through feedback both explicit and implicit—the designer is expected to progressively alter that experience to reflect the user's usage patterns, frustrations, successes, and unexpected by-products. In the language of digital products: iterate, iterate, iterate, and then iterate some more. Each iteration, each new version of the product, each newly added feature set is part of the conversation between the designer and the user. When an inveterate user of a digital product encounters a new change, she is listening to the object talk to her.

ALASKAN-BORN DESIGNER KEETRA DEAN DIXON HACKS, CONCEPTS, PROTOTYPES, AND PROBLEM SOLVES. "DELIGHT," SHE TELLS US. "BE BRAVE, VULNERABLE, AND CAPTIVATED BY THE UNREALISTICALLY FANTASTIC."[1] Dixon herself finds inspiration in the unexpected of the day-to-day. She harnesses technology to create wonder for others through experiences and artifacts. While in graduate school at Cranbrook Academy of Art she initiated her terrifying yet joyful process of taking on projects that require her to embrace the unknown. One such project, *The Museum as Manufacturer*, an installation at the Museum of Arts and Design in New York, demanded that she learn the ins and outs of 3-D printing, 3-D software, mechanism design, and construction—and how to hack into a garage-door opener. In another commissioned piece she emulated a generative computational process as she and her partner J. K. Keller swabbed layer after layer of hot wax on molded letterforms, a physical procedure in which they dwelled intensely on the letters before them. The result: a hundred-and-fifty-pound geode-like object that, when split open, revealed an opulent waxy message. Perhaps her determined spirit comes from the fact that she used to live in an igloo and fight bears for survival—or perhaps she just chooses not to live in fear of learning new things. The exquisite experiences and forms that emerge from the hands of Dixon and her collaborators attest that computation need not impede the expressive nature of humanity. Computation can magnify expression.

1 Tim Hoover and Jessica Heltzel, "Day 57," 100 Days of Design Entrepreneurship, *Kern and Burn*, April 30, 2015, http://www.kernandburn.com/the-book/one-hundred-days/day-57/. See also Tim Hoover and Jessica Heltzel, *Kern and Burn: Conversations with Design Entrepreneurs* (Baltimore: Kern and Burn LLC, 2013).

# MUSEUM AS MANUFACTURER

**KEETRA DEAN DIXON | 2013**

**DISRUPTIONS: A SLOWLY EVOLVING EXHIBIT OF DIGITAL ARTIFACTS REFLECTING THE DISRUPTIVE NATURE OF CONTEMPORARY EMERGENT TECHNOLOGIES AND UNANTICIPATED AUTHORSHIP.**

**DISRUPTIONS 1; DISRUPTIVE APPLICATION:**
Files that demonstrate the disruptive nature of 3-D printing.
—scalable prostheses
—adapter parts to allow different brands of children's construction toys to interconnect
—customizable product kits

**DISRUPTIONS 2; UNEXPECTED EVOLUTIONS:**
Digital files and physical output that demonstrate how the medium influences future form & function.
—influential structural restrictions and technological glitches
—physical translations of digitally native content

### DISRUPTIONS 3; AUTOPILOT AUTHORSHIP:

Featuring computational authorship and accidental collaborations resulting from unmanned influences and controls.
—forms produced by mathematic formula, biomimicry, genetic algorithms, and parametric software
—computational mergers of 3-D content shared through online resources

### DISRUPTIONS 4; OPEN + AUTOPILOT AUTHORSHIP + UNEXPECTED EVOLUTIONS + DISRUPTIVE APPLICATION

Building upon the previously explored themes, the MAD (Museum of Arts and Design in NYC) audience is invited to share 3-D digital content through an online exchange. Democratized content will be filtered, united, and transformed computationally before being manufactured onsite and displayed in the Museum as Manufactures collection.

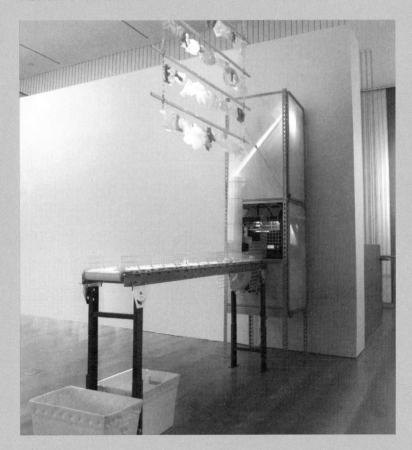

LEARN HOW TO DELIGHT PEOPLE, PARTICULARLY WHEN THEY DON'T REQUEST IT. IF YOU CAN GIVE A GREAT GIFT, YOU CAN MAKE A GREAT EXPERIENCE. THINK OF THE TASK AS GIVING A PRESENT TO THE VIEWERS.

**KEETRA DEAN DIXON**
*Kern and Burn: Conversations with Design Entrepreneurs*
2013

**HAAKON FASTE THRIVES AT THE INTERSECTION OF DESIGN AND TECHNOLOGY.** Trained first in studio art and physics at Oberlin College, and then in perceptual robotics at the Sant'Anna School of Advanced Studies, Faste puts human values at the center of his research.[1] His work as a designer and an educator at California College of the Arts considers our path to a posthuman future: humans and machines working reciprocally to develop postevolutionary technologies such as superintelligence, mind-uploading, and robotic life. Designers, he insists, can play a positive role in guiding this journey. In the essay below a speculative world governed by a posthuman "synchronized and sentient technocultural mind" looms ominously. But Faste sees great potential. As he explains, "Technology is human, and alive. And life is beautiful."[2] What technological systems, he challenges his peers, can designers build to facilitate both self and social actualization, resulting in a world that enables all of humanity—and even posthumanity—to flourish?

1 Hans Moravec, "When Will Computer Hardware Match the Human Brain?" *Journal of Evolution & Technology* 1 (1998).

2 Zeynep Tufekci, "The Machines Are Coming," *New York Times*, April 18, 2015.

# POSTHUMAN-CENTERED DESIGN

**HAAKON FASTE | 2015**

3 Hans Moravec, "When Will Computer Hardware Match the Human Brain?" *Journal of Evolution & Technology* 1 (1998).

Futurist experts have estimated that by the year 2030 computers in the price range of inexpensive laptops will have a computational power that is equivalent to human intelligence.[3] The implications of this change will be dramatic and revolutionary, presenting significant opportunities and challenges to designers. Already machines can process spoken language, recognize human faces, detect our emotions, and target us with highly personalized media content. While technology has tremendous potential to empower humans, soon it will also be used to make them thoroughly obsolete in the workplace, whether by replacing,

4 Zeynep Tufekci, "The Machines Are Coming," *New York Times*, April 18, 2015.

displacing, or surveilling them.[4] More than ever designers need to look beyond human intelligence and consider the effects of their practice on the world and on what it means to be human.

The question of how to design a secure human future is complicated by the uncertainties of predicting that future. As it is practiced today, design is strategically positioned to improve the usefulness and quality of human interactions with technology. Like all human endeavors, however, the practice of design risks marginalization if it is unable to evolve. When envisioning the

5 Jennifer Mankoff, Jennifer A. Rode, and Haakon Faste, "Looking Past Yesterday's Tomorrow: Using Futures Studies Methods to Extend the Research Horizon," *Proc. ACM Conference on Human Factors in Computing Systems* (2013), 1629-38.

future of design, our social and psychological frames of reference unavoidably and unconsciously bias our interpretation of the world. People systematically underestimate exponential trends such as Moore's law, for example, which tells us that in ten years we will have thirty-two times more total computing power than today.[5] Indeed, as computer scientist Ray Kurzweil observes, "we won't experience one hundred years of technological advances in the twenty-first century; we will witness on the order of twenty thousand years of progress (again when measured by today's rate of progress), or about one thousand times greater than what was achieved in the twentieth century."[6]

6  Ray Kurzweil, *The Singularity Is Near: When Humans Transcend Biology* (New York: Viking, 2005).

Design-oriented research provides a possible means to anticipate and guide rapid changes, as design, predicated as it is on envisioning alternatives through "collective imagining," is inherently more future-oriented than other fields.[7] It therefore seems reasonable to ask how technology-design efforts might focus more effectively on enabling human-oriented systems that extend beyond design for humanity. In other words, is it possible to design intelligent systems that safely design themselves?

7  Paul Dourish and Genevieve Bell, "Resistance Is Futile: Reading Science Fiction Alongside Ubiquitous Computing," *Personal and Ubiquitous Computing* 18, no. 4 (2014): 769-78.

Imagine a future scenario in which extremely powerful computerized minds are simulated and shared across autonomous virtual or robotic bodies. Given the malleable nature of such superintelligences—they won't be limited by the hard-wiring of DNA information—one can reasonably assume that they will be free of the limitations of a single material body, or the experience of a single lifetime, allowing them to tinker with their own genetic code, integrate survival knowledge directly from the learnings of others, and develop a radical new form of digital evolution that modifies itself through nearly instantaneous exponential cycles of imitation and learning, and passes on its adaptations to successive generations of "self."[8] In such a posthuman future, the simulation of alternative histories and futures could be used as a strategic evolutionary tool, allowing imaginary scenarios to be inhabited and played out before individuals or populations commit to actual change.[9] Not only would the lineage of such beings be perpetually enhanced by automation, leading to radical new forms of social relationships and values, but the systems that realize or govern those values would likely become the instinctual mechanism of a synchronized and sentient "technocultural mind."

8  Jenna Ng, "Derived Embodiment: Interrogating Posthuman Identity Through the Digital Avatar," *Proc. International Conference on Computer Design and Applications,* vol. 2 (2010): 315-18. Sherry Turkle, *The Second Self: Computers and the Human Spirit* (New York: Simon & Schuster, 1984).

9  Nick Bostrom, "The Future of Human Evolution," in *Death and Anti-Death: Two Hundred Years After Kant, Fifty Years After Turing,* ed. Ch. Tandy (Palo Alto, CA: Ria University Press, 2004), 339-71.

10  Anthony Dunne and Fiona Raby, *Speculative Everything: Design, Fiction, and Social Dreaming* (Cambridge: MIT Press, 2013).

Bringing such speculative and hypothetical scenarios into cultural awareness is one way that designers can evaluate possibilities and determine how best to proceed.[10] What should designers do to prepare for such futures? What methods should be applied to their research and training? Today's interaction designers shape human behavior through investigative research, systemic thinking, creative prototyping, and rapid iteration. Can these same methods be used to address the multitude of longer-term social and ethical issues that designers create? Do previous inventions, such as the internal combustion engine or nuclear power, provide relevant historical lessons to learn from? If little else, reflecting on super-intelligence through the lens of nuclear proliferation and global warming throws light on the existential consequences of poor design.[11] It becomes clear that while systemic thinking and holistic research are useful methods for addressing

11  Nathan Shedroff, *Design Is the Problem: The Future of Design Must Be Sustainable* (Brooklyn: Rosenfeld Media, 2009).

existential risks, creative prototyping or rapid iteration with nuclear power or the environment as materials is probably unwise. Existential risks do not allow for a second chance to get it right. The only possible course of action when confronted with such challenges is to examine all possible future scenarios and use the best available subjective estimates of objective risk factors.[12]

Simulations can also be leveraged to heighten designers' awareness of trade-offs. Consider the consequences of contemporary interaction design, for example: intuitive interfaces, systemic experiences, and service economies. When current design methods are applied to designing future systems, each of these patterns can be extended through imagined simulations of posthuman design. Intuitive human-computer interfaces become interfaces between posthumans; they become new ways of mediating interdependent personal and cultural values—new social and political systems. Systemic experiences become new kinds of emergent posthuman perception and awareness. Service economies become the synapses of tomorrow's underlying system of technocultural values, new moral codes.

The first major triumph of interaction design, the design of the intuitive interface, merged technology with aesthetics. Designers adapted modernism's static typography and industrial styling and learned to address human factors and usability concerns. Today agile software practices and design thinking ensure the intuitive mediation of human and machine learning. We adapt to the design limitations of technological systems, and they adapt in return based on how we behave. This interplay is embodied by the design of the interface itself, between perception and action, affordance and feedback. As the adaptive intelligence of computer systems grows over time, design practices that emphasize the human aspects of interface design will extend beyond the one-sided human perspective of machine usability toward a reciprocal relationship that values intelligent systems as partners.[13] In light of the rapid evolution of these new forms of artificial and synergetic life, the quality and safety of their mental and physical experiences may ultimately deserve equal if not greater consideration than ours.[14]

Interaction design can also define interconnected networks of interface touchpoints and shape them into choose-your-own-adventures of human experience. We live in a world of increasingly seamless integration between Wi-Fi networks and thin clients, between phones, homes, watches, and cars. In the near future, crowdsourcing systems coupled with increasingly pervasive connectivity services and wearable computer interfaces will generate massive stockpiles of data that catalog human behavior to feed increasingly intuitive

12 Kenneth R. Foster, Paolo Vecchia, Michael H. Repacholi, "Science and the Precautionary Principle," *Science* 288 (2000): 979-81.

13 Gianmarco Veruggio, "The Birth of Roboethics," *Proc. ICRA 2005, IEEE International Conference on Robotics and Automation, Workshop on Robo-Ethics* (2005).

14 David Levy, "The Ethical Treatment of Artificially Conscious Robots," *International Journal of Social Robots* 1, no. 3 (2009), 209-16. Tufekci, "The Machines Are Coming."

learning machines. Just as human-centered design crafts structure and experience to shape intuition, posthuman-centered design will teach intelligent machine systems to design the hierarchies and compositions of human behavior. New systems will flourish as fluent extensions of our digital selves, facilitating seamless mobility throughout systems of virtual identity and the governance of shared thoughts and emotions.

Applying interaction design to posthuman experience requires designers to think holistically beyond the interface to the protocols and exchanges that unify human and machine minds. Truly systemic posthuman-centered designers recognize that such interfaces, while informed by the design of touchpoints along the interactive narratives of human potential, will ultimately manifest in the psychological fabric of posthuman society at much deeper levels of meaning and value. Just as today's physical products have slid from ownership to on-demand digital services, our very conception of these services will become the new product. In the short term, advances in wearable and ubiquitous computing technology will render our inner dimensions of motivation and self-perception tangible as explicit and actionable cues. Ultimately such manifestations will be totally absorbed by the invisible hand of posthuman cognition and emerge as new forms of social and self-engineering. Design interventions at this level will deeply control the posthuman psyche, building on research methodologies of experience economics designed for the strategic realization of social and cognitive value. Can a market demand be designed for goodwill toward humans at this stage, or does the long tail of identity realization preclude it? Will we live in a utopian world of socialized techno-egalitarian fulfillment and love or become a eugenic cult of celebrity self-actualization?

It seems unlikely that humans will stem their fascination with technology or stop applying it to improve themselves and their immediate material condition. Tomorrow's generation faces an explosion of wireless networks, ubiquitous computing, context-aware systems, intelligent machines, smart cars, robots, and strategic modifications to the human genome. While the precise form these changes will take is unclear, recent history suggests that they are likely to be welcomed at first and progressively advanced. It appears reasonable that human intelligence will become obsolete, economic wealth will reside primarily in the hands of superintelligent machines, and our ability to survive will lie beyond our direct control. Adapting to cope with these changes, without alienating the new forms of intelligence that emerge, requires transcending the species limitations of human-centered design. Instead, a new breed of posthuman-centered designer is needed to maximize the inclusive potential of post-evolutionary life.

# Introducing the Election Technology Framework—
## Because We All Deserve a Better Voting Experience

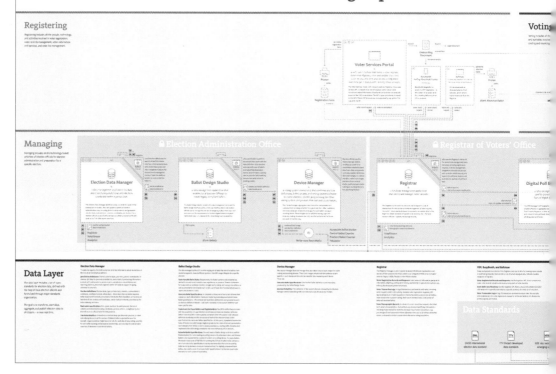

**KHOI VINH** Wildcard, 2014. Vinh teamed up with Steve Meszaros to create this browser. A reflection of Vinh's expertise in networked communication systems, Wildcard uses an emerging interaction paradigm: cards. Cards are single units of content or functionality, presented in a concise visual format that resembles a real-world playing card or postcard. They pull only what users need from the Web, creating a faster, mobile-optimized environment.

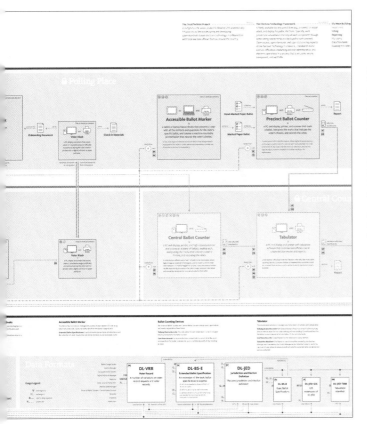

*opposite:* **DUBBERLY DESIGN OFFICE** Visualization of the TrustTheVote Election Technology Framework, 2014. The mission of the TrustTheVote Project is to develop trustworthy, up-to-date, complete election technologies and make these technologies available on an open-source basis for adoption by U.S. election jurisdictions. Working with the Open Source Election Technology Foundation, Dubberly Design Office is documenting and designing components of this project.

*left:* VoteStream, one of the first pieces of the project to be built, turns elections data into open data. Through this work Dubberly supports the larger trend of urging governments to release information, thus enabling insights to improve the current system.

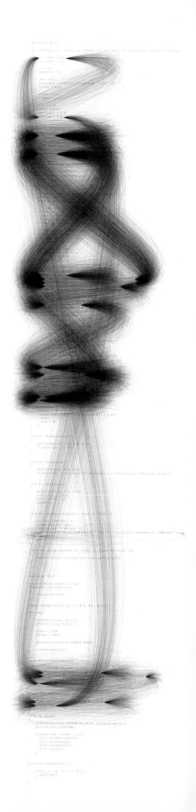

*above:* **CASEY REAS**
*A Mathematical Theory of Communication,* 2014. Reas plays with the information continually circling us—in radio waves, microwaves, satellites, etc.—by using an algorithm to transform the information into thousands of unique images. This project takes its title from Claude Shannon's article, "A Mathematical Theory of Communication."

*right:* **BEN FRY** *Deprocess,* 2006. An update to *Disarticulate,* 2004, this was created for the Processing installation at the 2006 Cooper-Hewitt Design Triennial. Fry visually interprets the sequence and repetition of code from *Articulate,* 2003, a project by Reas.

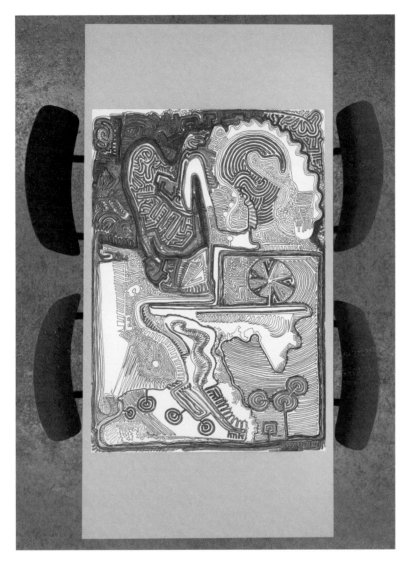

**CONDITIONAL DESIGN**
*Four Long Lines,* 2009. For this experiment, the members of Conditional Design followed these rules: Draw one line for an hour and a half without lifting your pen from the paper. You may stop for a maximum of five seconds, but the pen may not leave the paper. Don't cross another line.

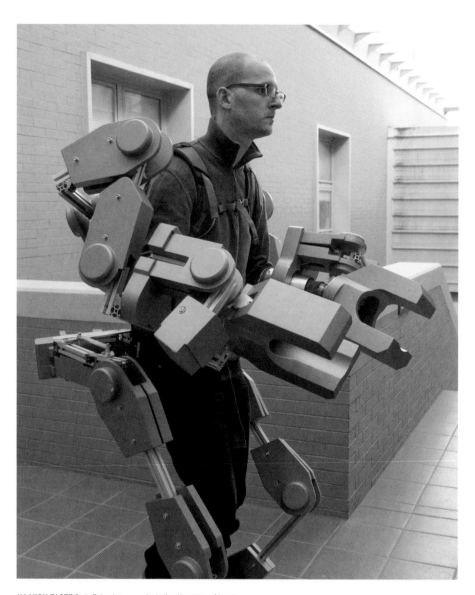

**HAAKON FASTE** Body Extender, PERCRO Perceptual Robotics Laboratory, Scuola Superiore Sant'Anna, Pisa, Italy, 2007–10. Exoskeletal robots can be used to convey sensations of force during teleoperation or virtual-manipulation procedures. Well-implemented robotic interfaces provide fully immersive and believable interaction with virtual or teleoperated worlds, including the sense of touch, force feedback, and presence in that world. They also provide intuitive perception of the robot as an extension of the user's body and mind, and thus a direct tool by which to examine the mechanisms of human cognition. This in turn may be used in the development of more intelligent interface systems that are capable of perceiving and learning autonomously.

clockwise from top left: **KEETRA DEAN DIXON** Lettering for the *New York Times Sunday Book Review*, 2014. Dixon generated patterning between letterforms within Illustrator using JavaScript, then finessed by hand.

**KEETRA DEAN DIXON** *Create React*, 2015. Dixon developed generative patterning with JavaScript, then applied it to letterforms.

**KEETRA DEAN DIXON** Editorial lettering outtake, 2015. Dixon formed connections between vertices in Illustrator with JavaScript. She unified and colored choice shapes manually.

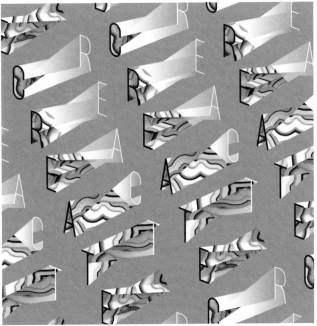

EMBRACE
THE

**KEETRA DEAN DIXON**
*Amazing Mistake,* a collaboration
with J. K. Keller, 2010. Dixon uses
JavaScript within Adobe Illustrator
to speed the creation of maximum
form and amplify some of Illustrator's
inherent aesthetics. In this case, she
applies the blend tool to letterforms
that have been fractured and randomly
colored with scripts.

# GLOSSARY

**ALLIANZ GROUP:** Founded in 1937, this group of Swiss artists and designers—including Max Bill, Max Huber, Leo Leuppi, and Richard Paul Lohse—championed principles of concrete art.

**ATOMS TO BITS:** This term, popularized by Chris Anderson, references new fabrication techniques and customized manufacturing that allow digital information to take physical form. The decreasing cost of technology, along with emerging production methods, now propels innovation in the physical as well as the digital world.

**AVANT-GARDE:** Driven by utopian visions, avant-garde artists of the early twentieth century, particularly those discussed in the context of graphic design, sought visual forms capable of objective, universal communication. These artists attempted to radically alter their societies by merging art with everyday life, shifting the arts away from the individual, subjective, and, in their minds, corrupt visions of the past.

**BAUHAUS:** Under the leadership of Walter Gropius, this influential school opened in Weimar, Germany, in 1919. Initially, its express purpose was to merge art and craft, thereby elevating German industrial design. Although the experimental work there varied greatly, graphic designers usually focused on efforts by prominent Bauhaus members, including László Moholy-Nagy and Herbert Bayer, to uncover a universally comprehensible visual language. This quest greatly influenced New Typography and ultimately the development of the grid system. Also of note is the Bauhaus Vorkurs, or basic course, which became a curriculum model for art and design schools internationally and particularly in the United States. More generally, the Bauhaus has become synonymous with high modern design.

***THE CATHEDRAL AND THE BAZAAR:*** In 1997 computer scientist Eric S. Raymond first published this influential text that examines the open-source, collaborative development methods used in the Linux project. His lessons for successful open-source software development (e.g., "Given a large enough beta-tester and co-developer base, almost every problem will be characterized quickly and the fix obvious to someone") increasingly permeate the creative process of graphic designers, interface designers, and industrial designers as widespread connectivity and rapid-prototyping tools incite makers to seek collaborative and open design models.

**CONCEPTUAL ART:** Sol LeWitt, one of the founders of the conceptual art movement, defined the movement as follows in a 1967 article for *Art Forum*: "In conceptual art the idea or concept is the most important aspect of the work. When an artist uses a conceptual form of art, it means that all of the planning and decisions are made beforehand and the execution is a perfunctory affair. The idea becomes a machine that makes the art." Conceptual art's separation between the concept/planning and the execution of a project influenced a generation of new media artists and designers, including Ben Fry and Casey Reas.

**CONCRETE ART:** Theo van Doesburg founded the group Art Concret in Paris in 1929. This movement advocates art that does not reference the natural world. Instead the components look to mathematics and geometry for inspiration. After World War II, Max Bill became a principal theorist of concrete art, spearheading a retrospective of the movement in Zurich in 1960.

**CONDITIONAL DESIGN:** Luna Maurer, Edo Paulus, Jonathan Puckey, and Roel Wouters founded this collective in 2008. Their manifesto presents three key components—process, logic, and input—of their work's emphasis on process over product.

**COPYLEFT MOVEMENT:** Advancing the free software movement, Richard Stallman led the way in developing new concepts of copyright that enable rather than limit the free distribution of information. Lawrence Lessig continued this tradition as a founding board member of Creative Commons, which advocates for flexible copyrights that allow content creators to reserve some rights but waive many restrictions on the reuse of information.

**EMIGRE:** Zuzana Licko and Rudy VanderLans founded *Emigre* magazine and, shortly thereafter, Emigre Fonts in 1984. Published until 2005, *Emigre* became an emblem of postmodern defiance of the streamlined, functional tenets of modernist design. Emigre Fonts established the frontier of digital type design, which coincided with the introduction of the Macintosh computer and PostScript technology.

**FREE SOFTWARE MOVEMENT:** Activist Richard Stallman founded the free software movement in 1983 with the launch of the GNU Project. In combination with Linux, the GNU Project became the first completely free software operating system, inspiring an ongoing commitment to mass collaboration among programmers, amateur and professional alike.

**GRID:** Grids divide and order content. They are most notoriously associated with International Style or Swiss style design. For practitioners of this influential design approach, complex, modular grids play a crucial role in the establishment of a tightly controlled design methodology. The grid's capacity to delineate specific design parameters for use by a wide range of designers forms a natural bridge between twentieth-century design theory and contemporary procedural thinking.

**HACKER MANIFESTO:** Loyd Blankenship (aka The Mentor) wrote "The Conscience of a Hacker" for the e-zine *Phrack* in 1986. The manifesto expresses the ideological underpinnings of hacker culture: individuals driven by curiosity who hack to expose weakness and corruption in an existing system and support free access to information. "This is our world now…the world of the electron and the switch, the beauty of the baud. We make use of a service already existing without paying for what could be dirt cheap if it wasn't run by profiteering gluttons, and you call us criminals. We explore…and you call us criminals. We seek after knowledge…and you call us criminals."

**INTERNATIONAL STYLE:** This design ideology stems from a modernist, rational, systematic approach. Its practitioners often use a limited typographic and color palette, carefully constructed modular grids, and objective imagery. Such designers put aside personal vision and become, instead, translators who clearly, objectively communicate the client message. This "valueless" approach helped professionalize the design field in the 1950s and '60s, moving it away from the arts and into the semi-scientific realm. Such systems were particularly useful for large-scale corporate identities that began to appear during that time.

**INTERNET OF THINGS (IoT):** Also referred to as ubiquitous computing, this term references a network of distributed objects embedded with sensors and other electronics. These objects transform from dumb objects to smart objects as they gather information and feed into a larger body of knowledge on the Internet. The objects begin to speak to one another, the manufacturer and/or user, creating highly efficient, data-driven automated systems. Technology pioneer Kevin Ashton, founder of the Auto-ID Labs at MIT, first used the term in 1999.

**MACINTOSH:** In 1984 Steve Jobs released the original Macintosh computer to the public. The Mac's accessible graphical user interface inspired countless young designers to begin experimenting with computation. Designer Susan Kare created typefaces and icons for its original operating system, including the Chicago typeface and the now ubiquitous trash can and system-error bomb icons.

**MASS PRODUCTION:** This production model results in large quantities of standardized products. The system is based on the premise that the per-unit cost goes down as the overall quantity goes up. Designers invest a great deal of time perfecting products before they are mass-produced. The system requires large up-front investment, storage, and distribution facilities.

**MODERNISM:** The modernist movement falls roughly between the 1860s and the 1970s. It is typically defined as artists' attempt to cope with a newly industrialized society. Modernism is progressive and often utopian, empowering humans to improve or remake their environments. Within modernism fall various other movements crucial to the development of graphic design. These include futurism, constructivism, and New Typography. The design community continues to debate the value of modernism, while basic modernist tenets still define conventional standards for effective design

**NANOTECHNOLOGY:** Rather than reshaping established materials from without, can we instead manipulate matter itself on an atomic, molecular, and supramolecular level? Designers consider nanotechnology in relation to principles of self-assembly and self-organization. As Paola Antonelli notes in "Design and the Elastic Mind": "The idea that you would only need to give the components of an object a little push for the object to come together and reorganize in different configurations could have profound implications for the environment."

**NEW TENDENCIES:** This movement, falling between 1961 and 1978, encompassed artists, designers, engineers, and scientists who explored possible applications of the computer as an artistic tool that could bridge art and science and thereby improve our society. The focus of the movement shifted over time from computers and visual research to computer art. The organizers chose to center the movement in Zagreb, Croatia, as a protest against the co-option of computer-inspired art by the commercial art scene of the United States and Western Europe.

**NEW WAVE:** Often used interchangeably with postmodernism or late modernism, this movement is often associated with Wolfgang Weingart, a leader of the second wave of Swiss style typography. Weingart rebelled against the Swiss design luminaries of the 1950s and '60s, pushing intuition and personal expression to the forefront of his work. Notable students are April Greiman and Dan Friedman. Greiman's particular brand of postmodernism often involved forays into new technology.

**OPEN SOURCE MOVEMENT:** Open source advocates are committed to free access to the source code of a computer program. Such access makes large-scale collaborative development models possible. Activist Richard Stallman's free software movement, founded in 1983, the copyleft movement, which began around the same period, and activist Lawrence Lessig's related Creative Commons licenses made the growth of the open source movement possible by resisting traditional twentieth-century copyrights, which prevent programmers from sharing resources.

**PARTICIPATORY DESIGN:** Participatory design requires the user to contribute content to the design project either during the ideation stage or through involvement with the design deliverable itself. Users increasingly expect some level of participation when they engage with content.

**PEER PRODUCTION:** This practice is defined by a large-scale collaborative production process that utilizes communities of self-organizing individuals. Peer production relies upon the networked-information economy and to some extent the free circulation of information.

**POSTHUMAN:** The term refers to a historical period in which artificial intelligence surpasses human intelligence. It is the linchpin of the paradigm emerging in this century, wherein computers, not humans, dominate the power hierarchy.

**POSTMODERNISM:** Adherents to this ideological paradigm recognize that meaning is inherently unstable; there is no essence or center that one should strive to reach. Broadly speaking, the term is closely associated with poststructuralism. Within the design community it can be used to refer to a layered, complex style or a poststructuralist critical approach to design. The postmodern movement begins roughly in the 1960s. There is no definite end point, although most suggest we have already moved past the postmodern world. Critics describe postmodernism as either a reaction against or the ultimate continuation of modernism. Either way, postmodernism moves away from the quest for absolutes and universally applicable values that characterize modernism.

**PROCEDURAL THINKING:** The process of breaking down problems and solutions into a formula that can be carried out by an information-processing agent (a human, a machine, or a combination of both).

**PROCESSING:** A programming language, development environment, and online community that encourages artists to actively engage with code and technologists to explore visual literacy. Ben Fry and Casey Reas developed the initial infrastructure of Processing in 2001 while enrolled in the MIT Media Lab within John Maeda's Aesthetics and Computation research group. Using an open-source model, they released their software to the community for further development. Processing remains freely accessible and open source.

**TECHNOLOGICAL SINGULARITY:** Science fiction writer Vernor Vinge popularized this term, which was originally used by mathematician John von Neumann in 1958. However, it is futurist Raymond Kurzweil who has in recent years spread awareness of the Singularity. Kurzweil predicts that by 2045, the acceleration of information-based technologies will have led to nonbiological intelligence that exceeds human intelligence.

# TEXT SOURCES

**22** Ladislav Sutnar, *Visual Design in Action: Principles, Purposes* (New York: Hastings, 1961).

**28** Bruno Munari, *Arte programmata. Arte cinetica. Opera moltiplicate. Opera aperta.* (Milan: Olivetti Company, 1964).

**30** Karl Gerstner, "Programme as Computer Graphics," "Programme as Movement," "Programme as Squaring the Circle," in *Designing Programmes* (New York: Hastings House, 1964), 21-23.

**36** Ivan E. Sutherland, "The Ultimate Display," *Proceedings of the IFIP Conference* (1965): 506-8.

**39** Max Bill, "Structure as Art? Art as Structure?" in *Structure in Art and Science,* ed. György Kepes (New York: Braziller, 1965), 150.

**41** Stewart Brand, "Whole Earth Catalog Purpose and Function," *Whole Earth Catalog: Access to Tools* (Menlo Park, CA: Portola Institute, 1968): 2.

**42** Wim Crouwel, "Type Design for the Computer Age," *Journal of Typographic Research* 4 (1970): 51-59.

**48** Sol LeWitt, "Doing Wall Drawings," *Art Now* 3, no. 2 (1971): n.p.

**58** Sharon Poggenpohl, "Creativity and Technology," *STA Design Journal* (1983): 14-15.

**62** April Greiman, "Does It Make Sense?" *Design Quarterly* 133 (1986).

**64** Muriel Cooper, "Computers and Design," *Design Quarterly* 142 (1989): 4-31.

**72** Zuzana Licko and Rudy VanderLans, "Ambition/Fear," *Emigre* 11 (1989): 1.

**75** Alan Kay, "User Interface: A Personal View," in *The Art of Human-Computer Interface Design,* ed. Brenda Laurel (Boston: Addison-Wesley, 1990), 191-207.

**82** Erik van Blokland and Just van Rossum, "Is Best Really Better," *Emigre* 18 (1990).

**86** P. Scott Makela, "Redefining Display," *Design Quarterly* 158 (1993): 16-21.

**88** John Maeda, "End," in *Design by Numbers* (Cambridge: MIT, 1999), 251.

**98** Ben Fry and Casey Reas, "Processing…," in *Processing: A Programming Handbook for Visual Designers and Artists* (Cambridge: MIT Press, 2012), 1-7.

**106** Paola Antonelli, "Design and the Elastic Mind," in *Design and the Elastic Mind* (New York: MoMA, 2008), 19-24.

**111** Hugh Dubberly, "Design in the Age of Biology: Shifting from a Mechanical-Object Ethos to an Organic-Systems Ethos," *Interactions* 15, no. 5 (2008): 35-41.

**120** Luna Maurer, Edo Paulus, Jonathan Puckey, Roel Wouters, "Conditional Design Manifesto," *Conditional Design*, May 1, 2015, http://conditionaldesign.org/manifesto/.

**122** Brenda Laurel, "Designed Animism," in *(Re)Searching the Digital Bauhaus* (New York: Springer, 2009), 251-74.

**126** Khoi Vinh, "Conversations with the Network," in *Talk to Me: Design and Communication Between People and Objects,* ed. Paola Antonelli (New York: MoMA, 2011), 128-31.

**132** Keetra Dean Dixon, "Museum as Manufacturer," Fromkeetra.com, May 1, 2015, http://fromkeetra.com/museum-as-manufacturer/.

# BIBLIOGRAPHY

## STRUCTURING THE DIGITAL

Alexander, Christopher. *Notes on the Synthesis of Form*. Cambridge: Harvard University Press, 1964.

Bill, Max. *Form: A Balance Sheet of Mid-Twentieth-Century Trends in Design*. New York: Wittenborn, 1952.

Bill, Max, Gerd Fleischmann, Hans Rudolf Bosshard, and Christoph Bignens. *Max Bill: Typografie, Reklame, Buchgestaltung = Typography, Advertising, Book Design*. Zürich: Niggli, 1999.

Bosshard, Hans Rudolf. "Concrete Art and Typography." In *Typography, Advertising, Book Design*. Zurich: Niggli, 1999.

Brand, Stewart, ed. *Whole Earth Catalog: Access to Tools*. Menlo Park, CA: Portola Institute, 1970.

Brook, Tony, and Adrian Shaughnessy, eds. *Wim Crouwel: A Graphic Odyssey*. Tokyo: BNN Inc., 2012.

Crouwel, Wim. *Kunst + Design: Wim Crouwel*. Ostfildern: Edition Cantz, 1991.

Fetter, William A. *Computer Graphics in Communication*. New York: McGraw-Hill, 1965.

Fuller, R. Buckminster. *Operating Manual for Spaceship Earth*. New York: Simon & Schuster, 1969.

Gerstner, Karl. *Compendium for Literates: A System of Writing*. Cambridge: MIT Press, 1974.

Gerstner, Karl. *The Forms of Color: The Interaction of Visual Elements*. Trans. Dennis A. Stephenson. Cambridge: MIT Press, 1986.

Gioni, Massimiliano, and Gary Carrion-Murayari, eds. *Ghosts in the Machine*. New York: Rizzoli, 2012.

Heller, Steven. "Sutnar & Lönberg-Holm: The Gilbert and Sullivan of Design." In *Graphic Design Reader*. New York: Allworth Press, 2002.

Hill, Anthony, ed. *Data: Directions in Art, Theory and Aesthetics*. Greenwich, CT: New York Graphic Society Ltd., 1968.

Hollis, Richard. *Swiss Graphic Design: The Origins and Growth of an International Style, 1920–1965*. New Haven: Yale University Press, 2006.

Hüttinger, Eduard, ed. *Max Bill*. New York: Rizzoli, 1978.

Isaacson, Walter. *The Innovators: How a Group of Hackers, Geniuses, and Geeks Created the Digital Revolution*. New York: Simon & Schuster, 2014.

Knobloch, Iva, ed. *Ladislav Sutnar V Textech (Mental Vitamins)*. Prague: Nakladatelstvi KANT a Umeckoprumyslové museum v Praze, 2010.

Knuth, Donald E. *Computer Modern Typefaces*. Boston: Addison-Wesley, 1986.

Knuth, Donald E. *Digital Typography*. Stanford: CSLI Publications, 1999.

Kröplien, Manfred, ed. *Karl Gerstner: Review of 5x10 Years of Graphic Design, etc.* Ostfildern: Hatje Cantz Verlag, 2001.

LeWitt, Sol. "Oral History Interview with Sol LeWitt." By Paul Cummings. *Archives of American Art*, July 15, 1974. http://www.aaa.si.edu/collections/interviews/oral-history-interview-sol-lewitt-12701.

LeWitt, Sol. "Paragraphs on Conceptual Art." *Artforum* 5, no. 10 (1967): 79–83.

Maldonado, Tomás. *Max Bill*. Buenos Aires: Editorial Nueva Visión, 1955.

Munari, Bruno. *Design as Art*. Trans. Patrick Creagh. London: Penguin, 1971.

Nelson, Theodor H. *Computer Lib: You Can and Must Understand Computers Now*. Chicago: Hugo's Book Service, 1974.

Price, Marla. *Drawing Rooms: Jonathan Borofsky, Sol LeWitt, Richard Serra*. Fort Worth: Modern Art Museum Fort Worth, 1994.

Rosen, Margit, ed. *A Little-Known Story About a Movement, a Magazine, and the Computer's Arrival in Art: New Tendencies and Bit International, 1961–1973*. Cambridge: MIT, 2011.

Sutherland, Ivan E. "Sketchpad, a Man-Machine Graphical Communication System," Doctoral dissertation, Massachusetts Institute of Technology, 1963.

Time-Life. "Toward a Machine with Interactive Skills." In *Computer Images 34*. Ann Arbor: University of Michigan, 1986.

Turner, Fred. *From Counterculture to Cyberculture: Stewart Brand, the Whole Earth Network, and the Rise of Digital Utopianism*. Chicago: University of Chicago Press, 2008.

Waldrop, M. Mitchell. *The Dream Machine: J. C. R. Licklider and the Revolution that Made Computing Personal*. New York: Viking, 2001.

Zevi, Adachiara, ed. *Sol Lewitt: Critical Texts*. Rome: Libri de AEIUO, 1995.

## RESISTING CENTRAL PROCESSING

Aldersey-Williams, Hugh, Lorraine Wild, Daralice Boles, and Katherine McCoy. *The New Cranbrook Design Discourse*. New York: Rizzoli, 1990.

Barthes, Roland. *Image-Music-Text*. London: Fontana, 1977.

Blackwell, Lewis. *The End of Print: The Graphic Design of David Carson*. San Francisco: Chronicle Books, 1995.

Brooks Jr., Frederick P. *The Mythical Man-Month: Essays on Software Engineering*. Boston: Addison-Wesley Professional, 1995.

Debord, Guy. *The Society of the Spectacle*. New York: Zone, 1995.

Derrida, Jacques. *Of Grammatology*. Baltimore: Johns Hopkins University Press, 1997.

Fella, Edward. *Edward Fella: Letters on America*. London: Lawrence King, 2000.

Foster, Hal, ed. *The Anti-Aesthetic: Essays on Postmodern Culture*. New York: New Press, 1998.

Foster, Hal, ed. *Postmodern Culture*. London: Pluto Press, 1985.

Friedman, Dan. *Dan Friedman: Radical Modernism*. New Haven: Yale University Press, 1994.

Gay, Joshua, ed. *Free Software, Free Society: Selected Essays of Richard M. Stallman*. Boston: Free Software Foundation, 2002.

Greiman, April. *Hybrid Imagery: The Fusion of Technology and Graphic Design*. New York: Watson-Guptill, 1990.

Hamm, Steve. *The Race for Perfect: Inside the Quest to Design the Ultimate Portable Computer*. New York: McGraw Hill, 2009.

Harvey, David. *The Condition of Postmodernity: An Enquiry into the Origins of Cultural Change*. Cambridge, MA: Blackwell, 1990.

Hofstadter, Douglas R. *Gödel, Escher, Bach: An Eternal Golden Braid*. New York: Basic Books, 1999.

Kostelanetz, Richard. *A Dictionary of the Avant-Gardes*. New York: Routledge, 2001.

Laurel, Brenda, ed. *The Art of Human-Computer Interface Design.* Boston: Addison-Wesley, 1990.

Levy, Steven. *Insanely Great: The Life and Times of Macintosh, the Computer that Changed Everything.* London: Penguin, 2000.

Lupton, Ellen, and Abbott Miller. *Design Writing Research: Writing on Graphic Design.* New York: Kiosk, 1996.

Lyotard, Jean-François. *The Postmodern Condition: A Report on Knowledge.* Manchester: Manchester University Press, 1984.

Makela, P. Scott, and Laurie Haycock Makela. *Whereishere: A Real and Virtual Book.* Berkeley: Gingko Press, 1998.

McLuhan, Marshall, and Quentin Flore. *The Medium Is the Message: An Inventory of Effects.* Corte Madera, CA: Ginko Press, 2001.

Miller, J. Abbott. *Dimensional Typography: Case Study on the Shape of Letters in a Virtual Environment.* New York: Princeton Architectural Press, 1996.

Negroponte, Nicholas. *Being Digital.* New York: Knopf, 1995.

Norris, Christopher. *Deconstruction: Theory and Practice.* New York: Routledge, 1991.

Poynor, Rick. *No More Rules: Graphic Design and Postmodernism.* New Haven: Yale University Press, 2003.

Raymond, Eric S. T*he Cathedral and the Bazaar: Musings on Linux and Open Source by an Accidental Revolutionary.* Sebastopol, CA: O'Reilly Media, 1999.

Rock, Michael. "P. Scott Makela Is Wired." *Eye* 12 (1994): 26–35.

Ronell, Avital. *The Telephone Book: Technology, Schizophrenia, Electric Speech.* Lincoln: University of Nebraska Press, 1989.

VanderLans, Rudy, and Zuzana Licko. *Emigre: Graphic Design into the Digital Realm.* New York: Van Nostrand Reinhold, 1993.

Weingart, Wolfgang. *Typography.* Baden: Lars Müller, 2000.

## ENCODING THE FUTURE

Anderson, Chris. *Free Culture: How Big Media Uses Technology and the Law to Lock Down Culture and Control Creativity.* New York: Penguin, 2004.

Anderson, Chris. *Makers: The New Industrial Revolution.* New York: Crown, 2012.

Armstrong, Helen, ed. *Graphic Design Theory: Readings from the Field.* New York: Princeton Architectural Press, 2009.

Armstrong, Helen, and Zvezdana Stojmirovic. *Participate: Designing with User-Generated Content.* New York: Princeton Architectural Press, 2011.

Benkler, Yochai. *The Wealth of Networks: How Social Production Transforms Markets and Freedom.* New Haven: Yale University Press, 2006.

Blauvelt, Andrew, and Koert van Mensvoort. *Conditional Design: Workbook.* Amsterdam: Valiz, 2013.

Bohnacker, Hartmut. *Generative Design: Visualize, Program, and Create with Processing.* New York: Princeton Architectural Press, 2012.

Brand, Stewart. *Whole Earth Discipline: Why Dense Cities, Nuclear Power, Transgenic Crops, Restored Wildlands, and Geoengineering Are Necessary.* New York: Viking, 2009.

Cormen, Thomas H., and Charles E. Leiserson. *Introduction to Algorithms.* Cambridge: MIT Press, 2009.

Dunne, Anthony, and Fiona Raby. *Speculative Everything: Design, Fiction, and Social Dreaming.* Cambridge: MIT Press, 2013.

Fry, Ben, and Casey Reas. "Processing: Programming for Designers and Artists." *Design Management Review* (2009): 52–58.

Fuller, Matthew. *Behind the Blip: Essays on Software Culture.* New York: Autonomedia, 2003.

Fuller, Matthew, ed. *Software Studies: A Lexicon.* Cambridge: MIT Press, 2008.

Graham, Paul. *Hackers and Painters: Big Ideas from the Computer Age.* Sebastopol, CA: O'Reilly, 2004.

Greenfield, Adam. *Everyware: The Dawning Age of Ubiquitous Computing.* Berkeley: New Riders, 2006.

Hunt, Andrew, and David Thomas. *The Pragmatic Programmer: From Journeyman to Master.* Boston: Addison-Wesley Professional, 1999.

Jenkins, Henry, Sam Ford, and Joshua Green. *Spreadable Media: Creating Value and Meaning in a Networked Culture.* New York: NYU Press, 2013.

Johnson, Steven. *Emergence: The Connected Lives of Ants, Brains, Cities, and Software.* New York: Scribner, 2002.

Knuth, Donald E. *The Art of Computer Programming.* Boston: Addison-Wesley Professional, 2011.

Laurel, Brenda. *Computers as Theatre.* Boston: Addison-Wesley Professional, 2013.

Laurel, Brenda. *Utopian Entrepreneur.* Cambridge: MIT Press, 2001.

Laurel, Brenda, and Peter Lunenfeld. *Design Research: Methods and Perspectives.* Cambridge: MIT Press, 2003.

Lessig, Lawrence. *Free Culture: The Nature and Future of Creativity.* New York: Penguin Books, 2005.

Levy, Steven. *Hackers: Heroes of the Computer Revolution.* Sebastopol, CA: O'Reilly Media, 2010.

Lunenfeld, Peter. *The Secret War Between Downloading & Uploading: Tales of the Computer as Culture Machine.* Cambridge: MIT Press, 2011.

Lupton, Ellen. *Type on Screen: A Critical Guide for Designers, Writers, Developers & Students.* New York: Princeton Architectural Press, 2014.

Maeda, John. *Maeda @ Media.* New York: Rizzoli, 2000.

Maeda, John. *The Laws of Simplicity (Simplicity: Design, Technology, Business, Life).* Cambridge: MIT Press, 2006.

Malloy, Judy, ed. *Women, Art, and Technology.* Cambridge: MIT Press, 2003.

Myers, William, ed. *Bio Design: Nature + Science + Creativity.* New York: Museum of Modern Art, 2014.

Nelson, Theodor H. *Designing Interactions.* Cambridge: MIT Press, 2007.

Pearson, Matt. *Generative Art: A Practical Guide Using Processing.* Shelter Island, NY: Pearson Education, 2010.

Petzold, Charles. *Code: The Hidden Language of Computer Hardware and Software.* Redmond, WA: Microsoft Press, 2001.

Poggenpohl, Sharon, and Keiichi Sato, eds. *Design Integrations: Research and Collaboration.* Bristol, UK: Intellect, 2009.

Reas, Casey, Chandler McWilliams, and LUST. *Form + Code in Design, Art and Architecture.* New York: Princeton Architectural Press, 2010.

Reas, Casey, and Ben Fry. *Getting Started with Processing.* Sebastopol, CA: Maker Media, 2010.

Rose, David. *Enchanted Objects: Design, Human Desire, and the Internet of Things.* New York: Scribner, 2014.

Salen, Katie, and Eric Zimmerman, eds. *The Game Design Reader: A Rules of Play Anthology.* Cambridge: MIT Press, 2006.

Sterling, Bruce. *Shaping Things.* Cambridge: MIT Press, 2005.

Vinh, Khoi. *Ordering Disorder: Grid Principles for Web Design.* Berkeley: New Riders, 2010.

# PHOTO CREDITS

**Inside front and back covers** illustration by Keetra Dean Dixon

**27, 51** Ladislav Sutnar © Ladislav Sutnar, reprinted with the permission of the Ladislav Sutnar Family.

**49, 53** Sol LeWitt "Doing Wall Drawings" © Estate of Sol LeWitt/ Artists Rights Society (ARS), New York. Courtesy Paula Cooper Gallery, New York.

**50** Max Bill © 2015 Artists Rights Society (ARS), New York / SIAE, Rome.

**67, 91** Muriel Cooper, reprinted courtesy of Nicholas Negroponte.

**94** P. Scott Makela, reprinted courtesy of Laurie Haycock Makela.

# TEXT CREDITS

**22** Ladislav Sutnar, "The New Typography's Expanding Future," in *Visual Design in Action: Principles, Purposes.* © Ladislav Sutnar, reprinted with the permission of the Ladislav Sutnar Family.

**28** Bruno Munari, *Arte programmata.* © Alberto Munari. Reprinted courtesy of Alberto Munari.

**39** Max Bill, "Structure as Art? Art as Structure?," in *Structure in Art and Science.* © Jakob Bill for all texts by Max Bill. Reprinted with the permission of Jakob Bill.

**75** Alan Kay, "User Interface: A Personal View," in *The Art of Human-Computer Interface Design.* Reprinted by permission of Apple, Inc.

**48** Sol Lewitt, "Doing Wall Drawings." © Estate of Sol LeWitt/ Artists Rights Society (ARS), New York. Courtesy Paula Cooper Gallery, New York.

**64** Muriel Cooper, "Computers and Design," *Design Quarterly* 142 (1989). Reprinted courtesy of Nicholas Negroponte.

**86** P. Scott Makela, "Redefining Display," *Design Quarterly* 158 (1993). Reprinted courtesy of Laurie Haycock Makela.

**88** John Maeda, foreword by Paola Antonelli, *Design by Numbers,* 500-word excerpt. © 1999 Massachusetts Institute of Technology, by permission of The MIT Press.

**106** Paola Antonelli, "Design and the Elastic Mind," from *Design and the Elastic Mind.* New York: The Museum of Modern Art, 2008. © 2008, The Museum of Modern Art, New York.

**122** Brenda Laurel, Excerpt from "Designed Animism," in *(Re)searching the Digital Bauhaus,* by Thomas Binder, Jonas Löwgren, and Lone Malmborg. Reproduced with permission of Springer in the format Book via Copyright Clearance Center.

Special thanks to Erik van Blokland, Stewart Brand, Wim Crouwel, Keetra Dean Dixon, Hugh Dubberly, Haakon Faste, Ben Fry, April Greiman, Alan Kay, Zuzana Licko, Luna Maurer, Edo Paulus, Sharon Poggenpohl, Jonathan Puckey, Casey Reas, Just van Rossum, Ivan E. Sutherland, Rudy VanderLans, Khoi Vinh, and Roel Wouters for permission to reproduce their work.

# INDEX

## COLOPHON

**BOOK DESIGNER:** Helen Armstrong

**VISUAL FOREWORD:** Keetra Dean Dixon

**EDITOR:** Nicola Brower, Princeton Architectural Press

**TYPOGRAPHY:** Interstate designed by Tobias Frere-Jones, 1993;
Seria designed by Martin Majoor, 2000.

## ABOUT THE AUTHOR

Helen Armstrong views design from across the spectrum as a
practicing designer, college professor, and published author. She is
an associate professor of graphic design at North Carolina State University. In addition to teaching, she wrote *Graphic Design Theory: Readings
from the Field* (Princeton Architectural Press, 2009) and cowrote, with
Zvezdana Stojmirovic, *Participate: Designing with User-Generated Content*
(Princeton Architectural Press, 2011). She also works as principal of
her own company, Strong Design. Her design work—for such clients as
Johns Hopkins, T. Rowe Price, and Euler ACI—has won regional and international awards. Her work has been included in numerous publications in
the United States and the United Kingdom, including *HOW International
Design Annual, The Complete Typographer,* and *The Typography Workbook.*